The
Pierce-Arrow
Showroom Is Leaking

The Pierce-Arrow Showroom Is Leaking

An Insider's View of the C.B.C.

Alex Barris

The Ryerson Press Toronto, Winnipeg, Vancouver

© Alex Barris 1969
Printed and bound in Canada
by The Ryerson Press Toronto
SBN 7700 0292 7
Library of Congress Catalog Card Number 72-97220

To Kay
Without whom I never want to be

FOREWORD

This book is not about automobiles, or buildings, or plumbing—even though all three are mentioned in the title. It is about television in Canada, particularly the CBC and particularly as seen through the eyes of one who has been involved in television for a dozen years.

The Pierce-Arrow Showroom is the "inside" nickname of a building in Toronto that has served as a CBC television studio for some fifteen years. The building is at 1140 Yonge Street, not far from some CPR tracks, in an area of which it might be said that both sides of the track are wrong. The history of the building may well be irrelevant. And yet one wonders if its shaky career might not somehow have left the building infected, so that future tenants would find it difficult to operate in it free of woes.

George N. Pierce, formerly a bird cage manufacturer in Buffalo, New York, built the first Pierce-Arrow in that city in 1904. It was a splendid car (even though its detractors promptly tagged it the "Fierce Sparrow") designed for the discriminating and priced for the affluent. For two decades, various Pierce-Arrow models were sold to gentlemen of means.

In 1927 the Pierce-Arrow Motor Car Company put up the building on Yonge Street in Toronto as a showroom for its elegant machines. It was a handsome structure for its time, with arched show windows and elaborately sculptured decorations. The architect was the late William Sparling, who the year before had built the Granite Club's posh new headquarters on St. Clair Avenue. Miss Merle Foster designed the sculpture, much of which still survives on the building's exterior.

Ironically, the building came too late. By 1927 the Pierce-Arrow company was experiencing serious financial difficulties, largely because the erstwhile bird cage manufacturer persisted in making high-priced quality cars that sold for anywhere from five to ten thousand dollars. Planned obsolescence not then being a common practice among automobile manufacturers, it was inevitable that in time the supply of luxury cars should exceed the supply of well-heeled sports. In 1928 Pierce-Arrow became a subsidiary of Studebaker but sales dwindled further, especially when North America plunged into the great Depression. In 1938 the Pierce-Arrow died quietly.

For a few years after it was built the Pierce-Arrow Showroom remained an automobile showroom, although the dealer (H. E. Givan Limited) branched out to other makes of car. In 1941 Givan gave up part of the premises to an engineering supplier and by 1943 he had moved out entirely, relocating farther downtown on Yonge Street. A series of other companies rented the building during the mid-forties and by the end of the war it was a vacant warehouse. The RCA Victor Company used the building for service and repairs for a few years. The CBC bought it in 1954.

CONTENTS

Foreword

The Pierce-Arrow Showroom Is Leaking   1

How To Break into Television   8

One of Our Stations Is Missing   17

Panelists and Panic   30

The Queen   43

Enter Private Enterprise   58

What Do You Do on Front Page Challenge?   68

Anatomy of a Failure   80

The No-Star System   91

The Games Producers Play   103

And Now a Word From—   117

The Saturday Night Problem   129

Who Reads the Critics?   150

Politics and Broadcasting   168

The CBC or — What?   185

The Pierce-Arrow Showroom Is Leaking

The executive offices of the Canadian Broadcasting Corporation in Toronto are located in a building on Jarvis Street known, not exactly affectionately, as the Kremlin. The nickname is not based on any physical resemblance to Russia's Kremlin; the CBC Kremlin has no onion-shaped domes or other exotic architectural splendors—it is, in fact, rather plain and square, as are some of its inhabitants. The Kremlin is separated from the CBC's main complex of studios by a parking lot and a few million light years. In twelve years of toiling for the Corporation, I have never once parked my car on that lot, which is reserved for staff members, from technicians to executives, but closed to actors, singers, musicians, writers and other free-lance riffraff.

The CBC's radio building and most of its television studios are situated in this same area. A feature of the radio building is the cafeteria in the basement. The staff of this cafeteria long ago discovered that most of its customers are performers in rehearsal, actors waiting to audition, writers waiting to see producers and announcers killing time between station breaks; since such people are too nervous to eat, no effort is made to serve anything even remotely appetizing.

The CBC has a sensible way of labelling studios. All radio studios are lettered, from A to about K. All television studios are numbered, from One to Seven. Thus, any visiting brass or MP's from Ottawa can always tell on the way in whether they are going to object to a radio or television program.

All but one of the CBC's Toronto television studies are in this complex, along with the radio building, the parking lot, the transmitter and the Kremlin. Studios One and Two, in the main TV building, are what you might call average 1952

1

television studios—too big to be wasted on newscasts, too small for most other shows. Studios Three, Five and Six (I think there's a Six, although I've never actually seen it) are in an annex, a sort of frame storehouse tucked behind the transmitter. These studios are ridiculously small and serve only for newscasts, static interviews and graffiti addicts. Studio Seven is the big one, behind the radio building and facing Mutual Street. It was built some years later than the others and reflects the Corporation's startling recognition that big shows sometimes need big studios. It is generally reserved for ballet, Festivals, king-size dramas, Wayne and Shuster programs and other large-scale "specials."

That leaves Studio Four, which isn't a bad idea. It is, perhaps significantly, located some considerable distance away from the main buildings, although not quite as far as you would expect Siberia to be from the Kremlin. It is on Yonge Street, at the corner of Marlborough, not far from a subway station and, more helpfully, a liquor store. Studio Four has its own parking lot, which I am also not entitled to use, but the commissionaires on duty there are less vigilant in their ejection of us unworthies, and I have on numerous occasions managed to pull into a space, lock up the car and hastily disappear into the building before a commissionaire could spot me.

Until Studio Seven was built, some nine years ago, Studio Four was the big one. It was used by Wayne and Shuster, Juliette, Bob Goulet, Shirley Harmer, Joan Fairfax, Gordie Tapp and other representatives of what might be termed loosely the Golden Age of CBC television. In fact, Studio Four is not so big. It is an absurd building: old, ugly, tired, obsolete but still used for many shows. As recently as the 1967/68 season, Studio Four was the home of Front Page Challenge, Flashback, the Tommy Hunter Show, In Person and Let's Go. Unlike Studios One, Two, Three, Five, Six (if there is one) and Seven, Studio Four was not built by the CBC. The Corporation, in its desperate need for more studio space back in the early 1950s, took over this barn and "converted" it into a TV studio. This is something like trying trying to turn Maple Leaf Gardens into Buckingham Palace without spending too much money.

Long before the CBC plunged into television (or even

radio) the building at Yonge and Marlborough was an automobile showroom, exhibiting at one time the shiniest new Pierce-Arrows. Studio Four is still sometimes referred to by some of us bitter veterans as The Pierce-Arrow Showroom. It is long and narrow—long enough and too narrow. It has a high ceiling and the acoustics of a sewer. Somewhere in the upper reaches of its dark heaven, the ghost of a vintage Pierce-Arrow klaxon hovers, waiting to laugh derisively at us for vainly thinking we could turn the auto palace into a studio. I have heard it now and then, mocking us.

Studio Four's appointments are, to be charitable, unpretentious. There is one dressing room for men, up a rickety staircase in the backstage area, and another for women, cleverly concealed between the make-up room and a wardrobe room. There is, incidentally, also a "star" dressing room at the other end of the building, but it is typical of the CBC that this is rarely used by a star, or even a pretender. There is something called a Green Room, which is a theatrical euphemism that comes in handy because to call it an Artists' Lounge would take gall. This is furnished with an abandoned board room table, a lumpy leather-covered sofa and some nondescript chairs, and yesterday's newspaper. The room is equipped with a TV monitor, presumably so that the artists can be aware of what is going on in the studio. This monitor has a marvelous sense of balance: one week you can get a picture on it, the next week you get sound—rarely both.

For programs that invite studio audiences, there are two sections of folding bleachers, calculated to make spectators as uncomfortable as possible. These are simply tiers of uncushioned wooden benches, backless and not notably roomy. The studio's control room used to be on the second floor at one end of the building. But since the advent of color TV, this has changed. The studio has color cameras, but they are part of a remote unit, which is removed every Saturday to cover the hockey games. When the remote truck control room is in use at Studio Four, it is parked inside the building, an inelegant reminder of the building's original function. But the old control booth on the second floor is still used for audio control, which merely tends to make things more difficult for the production staff. On the outside wall of this dingy building, facing Yonge Street, the bricked-up windows now serve as showcases for some truly awful paintings representing the programs that emanate from this glorious edifice. It is, all in all, a depressing place. It is depressing to think of all the programs that have been done there over the past years, each one having to compromise its intent to meet the niggardly specifications of the building. It is still more depressing to realize that this antiquated pile of rubble is still used to video-tape programs that are fed all across Canada. Most depressing is the prospect that the Pierce-Arrow Showroom will be in use a decade from now, its hard wooden bleachers still numbing the bottoms of docile spectators, its Green Room monitor still flipping over, its water fountain tap still propped open by a block of wood to keep the water cool, its dressing rooms still sporting half a dozen rusty wire coat hangers, its mechanical and structural limitations still crippling whatever creative inventiveness producers, writers, artists or choreographers might foolishly entertain in their scarred minds.

One of the series of programs done at Studio Four in the fall of 1966 was titled "A World of Music." It starred Malka and Joso, an international folk-singing duo of some repute who had been tapped to attempt the tricky transition from coffee house entertainers to television personalities. The program had been assigned the Saturday night network spot following the hockey games, the spot Juliette had held for ten years. This was the season when the CBC began televising programs in color and A World of Music was one of the first series to be done in color. The first three programs in the series were video-taped at various locations in Toronto in monochrome (that's TV talk for black and white) and then the program moved into Studio Four and the color era.

The program usually went in for sets with a European flavor—Spanish arches, middle-European Maypoles, Venetian fountains, et cetera—and six or eight appropriately costumed dancers filled in the visual background while Malka and/or Joso sang something from their substantial repertory of international songs. The show was video-taped on Wednesday nights at about 10:15. At first, studio audiences were used, but later it was decided that the space taken up by the bleachers could be put to better use (more arches, or gushier fountains) so the audiences were banished in favor of that most false device of the sham world of television, canned applause.

One particular Wednesday night has stayed with me, perhaps because its events crystalized the shameful inadequacy of Studio Four. After the day-long rehearsal, we broke for dinner. That was when we discovered it was raining heavily. When we returned from dinner, ready to start the dress rehearsal, I noticed something different about our set. To the arches and hanging artificial vines was added an incongruous note: buckets. Several buckets had been placed around the studio. The roof of the Pierce-Arrow Showroom was leaking and our colorful European set was being rained on. I could hear the klaxon laughing.

It was a demoralizing blow. You can get caught up in the illusions of television—not the image on the screen at home, but the illusions of working in the medium. You have cameras and sets and musicians and artists and craftsmen; you take some satisfaction in being a part of a dynamic medium; you are turning out variety programs, in color yet; you are helping to provide entertainment for people across Canada; you know the routine of it, the tricks of the trade, the excitement, the joy of seeing it all fall into place. You are a professional in a highly skilled field. And then, suddenly, you crash to earth. The whole illusion of professionalism, of the invigorating world of television production is destroyed by the realization that what you are working on is doomed to be second-rate—doomed by the inane conditions under which the illusions live and falter, doomed by a leaky roof.

The producer of the program, Mark Warren, promptly had his assistant, Caroll Wilson, call the maintenance department to report the crisis. She reported back that the maintenance department had duly noted our complaint and would look into it in the morning. She had patiently explained that we were due to video-tape a color television program in about an hour and that something had to be done about the leaky roof before morning—*now*. But that, of course, was not possible. Not only were maintenance crews off duty at that time of night, but there wasn't much they could do about fixing a leaky roof while it was still raining.

It's at moments like these that a producer's sanity is tested. He can, of course, cancel the taping—at a cost of several thousand dollars. As the writer of the show, I toyed with the idea of suggesting we take advantage of the indoor rain and, with only minor revisions, let our performers do a sort of European version of *Singin' in the Rain*. A little voice inside me wisely told me to shut up, thereby possibly saving Mark Warren from facing a murder rap.

Time and whatever guardian angel it is that watches over converted Pierce-Arrow showrooms saved us all. The ghost of the klaxon was foiled again. The dripping in the buckets began to slow down. About fifteen minutes before the taping was scheduled to start, the rain stopped and didn't start again that night. The show was taped and the home audience the following Saturday had no inkling that the program had almost been called on account of rain.

One reason I'm glad I'm not a CBC producer (perhaps the reason I could never be one) is that I was secretly sorry the rain had stopped. It's probably a flaw in my character, but sometimes I find myself wishing for a showdown. Had I been the producer, had the rain continued, I would have relished the showdown. I would (I like to think) have cancelled the taping and caused hell to be raised the next day over the failure of the maintenance department to provide us with the absolute minimum requirement for doing a TV show in a studio—a roof that doesn't leak. But I was not the producer, and the rain stopped, and the next day the incident of the leaky roof became nothing more than one of those weird show business anecdotes.

So, the showdown is averted, the show goes on. The roof is patched up, until next time. Thus, we limp along, from patch to patch, from show to show, from season to season, with ludicrously outdated equipment, with impossibly low budgets, with a Rube Goldberg studio, sometimes with lamentably unaware management, with public indifference, with sweeping press antagonism, with stopgap, nick-of-time solutions to acute problems, worst of all with not much hope that any long-range plan will be devised to meet the problems constantly faced by a television service that has for too long been the victim of the public's ignorance and the politicians' cynicism.

If it seems I'm making a federal case out of an isolated, insignificant, mildly amusing incident, maybe I've failed to state it clearly enough. I'm not picking on the CBC's maintenance department, nor any single CBC department, nor even the CBC itself, for that matter. The incident above, it seems to me, is a symptom of the lingering CBC malaise; it is one of many incidents that suggest there is something wrong about a huge corporation, charged with the staggering responsibility for providing a national television service in a vast, thinly populated country, and operating in an atmosphere of hostility, lack of understanding, crisis and chaos. The CBC consists of a lot of people apprehensively sticking fingers into a crumbling dike, distracted in their work by the expectation that the whole thing will crush them at any moment.

The Pierce-Arrow Showroom is leaking, and nobody is on duty. Perhaps the whole CBC is leaking, and nobody has a finger to spare. Or maybe nobody cares.

For the past dozen years, I have been involved in television, almost exclusively at the CBC, as writer and performer, often as voyeur to its rape. I have seen shows come to life, flourish, or flounder and die. I have attended at births and deaths. Much of it has been fun, much of it has been frustrating. But I have come to view the CBC as a dear old aunt, rather eccentric but beloved, one who does some nutty things, but who is nevertheless an integral part of the Canadian family, whose existence could be made happier and more meaningful with some help and some understanding.

I have two reasons for writing this book—three, if you count making a buck. One is to tell the reader a little bit of what life is like with Auntie Maimed, and what might be done to ease her suffering. The other is to tell you about some of the people in Canadian television and relate, as honestly as I can remember them, some of the crazy, mad, maddening, improbably bizarre, pathetic, frenetic, dramatic, infuriating, wild, unbelievable things that can go on in television, possibly anywhere, but specifically and certainly in Canada.

How To Break into Television

Dear Mr. Barris,

I am most anxious to play a part, however small, in the programs of the CBC.

I believe that somewhere, in some area of production or writing, there is a tiny niche for me—with just enough room to ventilate ideas and express myself.

It was a compulsion to write that. . . .

That's part of a letter that came to me one day last summer. I get a few of them, from time to time, and I am by no means unique in this. I know that virtually everyone connected with television or any other facet of the entertainment world gets them, too.

A woman from England, middle-aged, brash, energetic and with some little experience back home, keeps turning up or calling me to see if there is a place for her, on whatever program I happen to be connected with at the moment. The first time she called me, she tried to convince me that she was perfect for Flashback. At the first opportunity to break into her pitch, I informed her (with some relief) that I had no connection at all with Flashback but was the writer of Front Page Challenge. With barely a pause for breath, she began telling me how perfect she would be for Front Page Challenge.

A man I knew slightly spent weeks tracking me down for a meeting to discuss a television "project." Our meeting revealed that he had no clear idea of what he wanted to do, but he and a few of his friends felt certain that "we" could do a TV series. I was their unanimous choice to be the writer —even though they were very vague about what kind of writing would be involved. I have no notion, incidentally, if I was their first unanimous choice or their seventh. A woman with a teenage son who hadn't completed high school but was "loaded with personality" wanted to know from me how she could get him into television. She had no idea of what he might do but she was convinced he'd be great. A pianist I know is certain he has a flair for writing comedy. So does an ad agency man I've known for some years. So do several other musicians, actors, publicity men, newspapermen, secretaries, researchers, salesmen and students feel they belong in television. And then there are all those midwest housewives with hyphenated names and a love of poetry.

Some of these people may very well be right. Many more of them are dead wrong. It is not much of a tribute to television, I guess, that it appears to be so easy to so many people to contribute to its improvement. The man with the vague idea that he would like to be involved in the creation of a television series of some sort, or the woman with the difficult but personable teenage son will probably switch their dreams to some other apparently easy field—say, interior decorating or selling mutual funds.

There are, however, the more serious ones and it is not as easy to dismiss them. A film cameraman sent me a script for a feature film—just to get my opinion of it. He had written it, was naturally excited over it and was unswervingly convinced it could form the basis for a feature film industry in Canada. (This unlikely idea comes without warning into the minds of a dozen or so optimists a year, each of whom believes he has figured out some magic formula that never occurred to all the others.) In this case, I read the script carefully, but with mounting discomfort, and then sent it back with a letter telling him, as gently as I could, why I thought it wouldn't do. I don't know what his reaction was, but if he's human he probably dismissed me as a stuck-up nincompoop who doesn't have the sense to recognize a work of art when he sees it.

Over the years, I have watched many young entertainers or actors start from scratch, work hard, develop their talent, gain experience and begin working successfully in show business. But I have also seen others who take a fling at it and then get bored or find out they can't take the frustrations, the heartaches, the maddening success of others who seem less talented, or the emotional impact of setbacks. One runs into them sometimes; they are housewives or teachers or salesmen and they are probably better off—but they wouldn't believe that.

On the whole, I agree with the shrewd observation of Mama Rose, the mother of Gypsy Rose Lee in the musical based on that remarkable lady's career. Mama Rose spent her life pushing her two daughters onto the stage, frequently reminding them that she had sacrificed her own potential career for them. Late in the story, Gypsy, in a fit of compassion, soothes her embittered mother by telling her that she surely could have been a great star herself if she had worked for her own future rather than her daughters'.

"Na-a-ah," says Mama Rose philosophically. "If I could-a-been, I would-a been."

So. I suppose I've boxed myself into a corner and now I am expected to deliver one of those stirring sermons about how hard work, initiative, perseverance, clean living and possibly prayer are the ingredients for success in show business. Not quite. Let me tell you how I backed into television.

In the spring of 1955 I was a columnist for the *Globe and Mail*, in Toronto, covering movies, television, night clubs and anything else that might be classified as entertainment. I had been doing this sort of thing for about three years, after having spent several years as a reporter. My editor, the late Oakley Dalgleish, sent me on a most unusual mission to New York City. The previous summer, swimmer Marilyn Bell had conquered Lake Ontario, thereby becoming not only a national heroine but the darling of the Toronto afternoon papers. The *Telegram* and the *Star* trampled each other half to death in their zeal to tie her up for exclusive stories and pictures. Serenely, the *Globe and Mail* had stayed out of the squabble, beyond reporting the event. But Mr. Dalgleish was given to epic ideas. Nothing could be more appropriate, he reasoned, than that Marilyn Bell, the great Canadian athlete, should be a featured attraction at the Jones Beach water show presided over each summer by Guy Lombardo, an expatriate Canadian and, incidentally, onetime friend of the deceased publisher of the *Globe and Mail*, George McCullagh.

My mission, so help me, was to go to New York to persuade Mr. Lombardo of the wisdom of this brainstorm and also to negotiate the terms for Miss Bell. (I can only assume that Mr. Dalgleish and, therefore, I, had some authorization to act in this matter. Mr. Dalgleish felt no compulsion to confide such bothersome details to me.) After a lifetime of religiously avoiding Mr. Lombardo's saccharine music, I found myself staying at the Roosevelt Hotel, then his bailiwick, and subjected to great gobs of the sweetest music this side of Lawrence Welk for several evenings in a row. During the days, I even accompanied Guy and his brothers to a recording studio for more of the same, in hopes of finding a few spare moments to discuss my Big Deal.

An agreement was finally worked out. Mr. Lombardo had apparently retained enough of a spark of Canadianism to see the value of booking Miss Bell to swim in the Jones Beach show for a not astronomical fee. My mission, I guess, must therefore be regarded as having succeeded. However, the incident stayed in my mind for quite a different reason. On one of the evenings when I felt I could no longer stand Lombardo's music, I remained in my hotel room and watched television. What I watched in particular was the Tonight Show, then starring Steve Allen, which had begun some months before as a local New York program and had only recently been put on the NBC network.

It had the effect on me of making me wish I could do such a program in Canada. I felt no misgivings, I confess it quite brazenly, about my ability to do such a television program. What appealed to me most was the informality of it, the unpredictability, the feeling that this sort of program was the essence of television, in that it offered, in an entertaining way, real people rather than studied, rehearsed, slick, bloodless, one-dimensional actors, performers and announcers. It demonstrated, as nothing I had seen before, that television relied on people rather than sets, tricky camera work and the like. I didn't, at the time, think about the practicality of doing a similar program in Toronto. I knew relatively little about the mechanics of television, still less of the logistics. I suppose I was a little bit like some of those people who write those letters I mentioned earlier. However, I wasn't thinking in terms of a new career—it just seemed to me something worth doing which I felt I could do, if given the chance.

In any case, I returned to Toronto and to my daily coverage of the entertainment scene. A few weeks later I heard a rumor that the CBC was planning a late-night show somewhat along the lines of the Allen format. Until then, I had done virtually no television work—an appearance with Dick MacDougall on "Jazz with Jackson," an occasional interview on "Tabloid," some judging of talent on "Pick the Stars." But I had worked on radio, both at CBC and elsewhere, and I knew a few producers and executives in the CBC.

I called an executive whom I knew and said I'd heard a late-night program was in the planning stage and that I'd like to be considered as a candidate for the master of ceremonies job. He was rather patronizing, as if I were some disreputable storm window salesman who had somehow got past his secretary. He made it abundantly clear that I had not been considered and even managed to imply that the whole idea was mildly amusing. I tried, as tactfully as I could, to suggest to him that it really wasn't an altogether bizarre idea.

"Alex," he said, leaving the door open for some miracle he obviously didn't expect to occur, "if and when we find the right guy, it won't matter if he has two heads." I pulled my one and only head back into its shell and thanked him for his time. I heard no more about the proposed CBC show for a few months.

Perhaps I should explain that my interest in show business wasn't really born the first time I saw Steve Allen. When I was a child, I had a taste of it, doing a fair bit of semi-professional singing and acting, and I guess I was a bit stage-struck from those years. The business of growing up, going through a war and then having to earn a living had pretty well snuffed out any ambitions I might have had for a career in show business. But the interest was always there. A few years before this time, as a reporter for the *Globe and Mail*, I had been posted to the press gallery of the provincial legislature and was active in setting up an annual Press Gallery Show put on by the reporters for the members of the legislature. I wrote material for these shows, directed and appeared in several of them. They were, of course, amateur productions, but we had much fun in doing them.

In 1955 the Toronto Men's Press Club decided to institute what it called a Fall Ball, a sort of antidote to the big, sprawling Byline Ball staged by the club each spring. I became involved in preparing the entertainment for this first Fall Ball, working again with other newspapermen. I served as director and master of ceremonies for the show. By one of those coincidences that used to turn up in Alice Faye-Don Ameche movies, the aforementioned skeptical CBC executive was present—in a manner of speaking—when the entertainment was presented at the Toronto Men's Press Club Fall Ball.

Once again Marilyn Bell inadvertently enters the picture. I had written a parody (to the tune of Casey Jones) titled "The Ballad of Marilyn Bell," ribbing the newspapers over their extravagant coverage of the Lake Ontario swim and Marilyn's other exploits. Because it had special meaning for that largely press audience, the number was the hit of the show and, in fact, the whole show was well received. The CBC executive (who, it must be clear by now, shall remain nameless) was present, as I said, in a manner of speaking. In fact, he was quite drunk. Also present that night was a radio producer with whom I had occasionally worked at CBC. This fellow was impressed by my work as MC of the show and telephoned the executive the following Monday to suggest that some use might be made of me in television. As he later reported the conversation to me, the executive had admitted to him that he didn't remember seeing the show at all, let alone anyone in it.

Anyway, the long-talked-of late night show was just then beginning on CBLT, the Corporation's local Toronto station. It was called "Eleven Thirty Friday," this inspired title having been suggested by the fact that this was the time and day of each program. Rather than choosing a regular MC, the CBC was using different men each week—sort of on-the-air auditions. Among those I can recall seeing were Lister Sinclair and Byng Whitteker.

The radio producer told me he had persuaded the executive to "try Barris" on one show. A week or two later I received a call from Len Casey, who was producing Eleven

Thirty Friday. He asked me to drop in to see him, indicating he had "heard" that I was interested in "hosting" one of his shows. I went to see Casey, taking time first to set a few ideas down on paper—suggestions for what sort of program I'd like to do. We got along well enough and an agreement was reached that I would be host of one program, sometime in January. (Later, Casey told me that normally I would receive sixty dollars, which was then the union scale payment for a non-network hour show, but that because I was also writing the script he had managed to get this doubled, to a hundred and twenty dollars. It didn't strike me as a lavish sum for writing and hosting an hour television show, but I was anxious to have a crack at it, so the money seemed less important.)

The program went reasonably well. I had a few guest acts, did a couple of satirical bits and an interview with actor Anthony Quayle, who was then appearing in Toronto. In March, I did a second program, more or less along the same lines, and immediately after that Casey told me "they" wanted me to host a one-occasion hour long show, somewhat similar in style to the Eleven Thirty Friday series, except that it would be sponsored and be telecast on the CBC network in prime time. This was called "Encore" and was done in April, 1956. For this third (network) show my fee skyrocketed to two hundred dollars.

These three-hour shows were my introduction to light entertainment television at the CBC, and also to the business of working closely, as both writer and performer, with a CBC television producer. My TV education had begun. One of the things I learned was that producers, like everyone else, have their idiosyncrasies. Casey had once been a dance band musician, and the area of TV production in which he showed the greatest interest was, naturally enough, the music and its reproduction on the air. Consequently, when his Eleven Thirty Friday series was given an increase in budget—from peanuts to cashews, roughly—he spent it all on increasing the size of the orchestra (which was led by pianist Lou Snider), from eight men to sixteen. This struck me then (and now) as a rather frivolous way to use up all the extra money, but Casey didn't agree. To him, music and sound were paramount; to me, the musical portions of such a show should really have served as punctuation marks for the informal talk and light comedy. While it was certainly important that the music be good, I didn't think that type of program would stand or fall on whether it had an eight- or sixteen-piece band. But in Canadian television, at least, the producer bears the final responsibility for the success or failure of a show, and therefore has the power of decision. This is not always so in U.S. television. As to the pros and cons of each system, that's a matter to be examined more fully in a later chapter.

(Casey, incidentally, narrowly escaped a serious row over this whole business of the orchestra. For some reason, he and Lou Snider were not on especially good terms. When Casey decided on enlarging the band, he disapproved of the musicians Snider had chosen. Traditionally, this is a musical director's prerogative and the musicians' union jealously guards this jurisdiction. Casey imprudently told Snider which musicians he preferred and a blowup between the CBC and the union was just barely averted.)

The rift between Casey and Snider widened. When we were rehearsing the Encore show, the one that was to go on the network, it developed that Snider's music copyist had made some errors in some of the music; to correct the music and rehearse the orchestra again would require spending some money, which Casey's tight budget could ill afford. Snider acknowledged the responsibility for the errors, but Casey, apparently determined to prove to somebody or other that Snider was the wrong man for the job, refused to authorize payment of the extra money for additional rehearsal. This was on the day of the show—and in those days shows were done "live" rather than recorded on video-tape in advance of their telecast.

I got a little hot then and argued with Casey that it didn't seem very professional to me to allow a show to go on the air with known flaws that could still be corrected, simply to defend some sort of murky principle. Casey reluctantly gave in, but it was obvious that he and Snider could not continue working together much longer. In fairness to Casey, it should be stated that Lou Snider was clearly forced on him at the outset. If a producer is to be truly in charge, he should pick his own people. Shotgun weddings don't work any better on

TV than anywhere else. Whether Casey was right or wrong in not wanting Snider is beside the point.

What resulted from my two Eleven Thirty Friday shows and the Encore program was a proposal by the CBC that I "front" a summer replacement series, a half hour each week, roughly along the same lines—informal talk, some comedy and some music. Len Casey was to be the producer, but Lou Snider was not to be involved. Casey and I spent considerable time together in the next couple of months planning the series. Thus, without any long, hard, dedicated effort on my part I found myself up to here in television. I did not, of course, give up my job at the *Globe and Mail*. To do so on the strength of a thirteen-week series would have been foolhardy. But there was no conflict between the two jobs and my employers at the paper, while not notably enthusiastic about my delving into television, registered no objection.

What I've written here about my introduction to television is, as clearly as I can remember it, the way it happened. I mention this because I cannot claim to be any shining example of the virtue of perseverance. My interest in television was serious enough, of course, but had it never led to active participation in the medium I would simply have gone on writing for newspapers, magazines or whatever. I guess that's why those letters and calls from people aching to get into show business bother me. I know, better now than I did then, that there is no real substitute for ability, preparation, hard work, determination and a little bit of luck. Except sometimes, maybe, when the luck is more than a little bit—as in my case.

One of Our Stations Is Missing

Becoming involved in a weekly television series, I soon found out, can cause some lingering headaches. The CBC's publicity department, that dauntless depository of countless secrets, wanted pictures of me, as well as background information to send out to the press of the nation. Publicity men, even those employed in a government-financed corporation, always look for an "angle." In my case, because I was a newspaper columnist, I guess, I was painted as a kind of Damon Runyon character. Or maybe it was because I was born in New York. I don't really know. In an interview with one publicity man who was preparing a biography of me, I mentioned that I had done some singing as a child. Somehow this got twisted up in his notes and it came out, in the publicity release, that I had once been "a song-and-dance man" in New York.

That phrase still haunts me. Whenever anyone decides to write anything about me, out come the old newspaper clippings, this inaccuracy is again disinterred and I am referred to as an ex-song-and-dance man. I don't know why this should continue to irritate me—apart from the fact that it simply isn't true—but it does. (I am not alone in this, of course. Norman Jewison, once a CBC producer and now one of Hollywood's most gifted film directors, spent one summer of his youth driving a taxi in Toronto, simply because he needed a job. That was twenty years ago, but to this day one can find references in articles about Jewison to the "ex-cab driver turned director," as if he were some Brooklyn character who had simply parked his cab one night and began directing movie stars the next day.)

My program was to be called "The Barris Beat," a suggestion which, as I recall it, came from Len Casey, who was to produce the series. I liked the title and, in fact, used it as the name of my newspaper column when I moved from the *Globe and Mail* to the *Telegram* a year or so later. (At the *Globe*, my column had the singularly uninspired title of "Casting About with Barris," and I am certain that some people occasionally turned to it in hopes of finding tips on good fishing holes.) But I had no idea the name of my show would meet with resistance from the CBC. The man with whom I had to discuss it, as well as the whole matter of my doing the show, was Robert McGall, then the supervisor of light entertainment for the network. I was not yet then aware of the unofficial "no-star" policy of the CBC and, I suppose, it must have been awkward for McGall to convey this to me without actually stating it. In any case, he indicated that while the title sounded fine, it wasn't really acceptable. Naively, I said I couldn't see why.

"Well," he said, "suppose we do call this program 'The Barris Beat.' Then, after it's on the air for a few weeks or months, you step off a curb and a truck hits you. Now, I know that sounds terribly cold-blooded, but it could happen. We'd be forced to change the name of the show." The logic of this eluded me and I said so. If I were killed by a truck, I argued, the CBC would have to do something to replace the show, *whatever* its title was. He then said that it wasn't CBC policy to name shows after people; the Corporation preferred titles like "Holiday Ranch" and "Country Hoedown." But I cited some examples, like Billy O'Connor and Juliette, whose names were in the titles of their shows. Somewhat reluctantly, he agreed to let the title stand.

Before long, I was to learn that anonymity as a policy manifested itself in other ways, too. From the beginning, I was primarily responsible for writing the show, as well as "hosting" it. Yet, my producer, Len Casey, saw no necessity for giving me a writing credit at the end of the show, as I had seen given to writers on other shows. His argument, when we got around to discussing it, was that he too had a hand in preparing the script (which was true, to the extent that he could veto my ideas or ask that they be changed or edited) and by rights he should be getting a writing credit too. That was fine with me, so after about the third show the credits read:

"Written by Alex Barris and Len Casey."

My inexperience allowed me to get into a position which I later recognized as intolerable. Although it was some time later, it was again while I was working with Casey that the full impact of this error dawned on me. To this day, I cling to the belief that it is absolutely wrong for a producer to be involved as a co-writer on a show of which he is also the producer. From the standpoint of the other writer (me, in this case) it's a little bit like playing in a game in which your opponent is also the referee. Or, put another way, in any disagreement he has two votes to your one.

The Barris Beat started out as a Wednesday evening summer replacement series, with a number of permanent cast members besides myself. They included singers Betty Jean Ferguson and Roy Roberts, the Gino Silvi (vocal) Octet and Bill Isbister and his orchestra. In addition, there were such guests as Sammy Sales, Doug Romaine, Dave Broadfoot, Joey Hollingsworth and the Willy Blok Hansen dance trio. From the beginning, Sammy was particularly helpful in writing comedy material and also appearing in sketches. This warm, lovable man had had much experience in theatre and night club work. His understanding of comedy values was sound; and he wanted sincerely to see my show succeed. I was happy to have him on the team and from the beginning I felt he, too, should have a writing credit, but the producer disagreed.

Almost from the beginning, I discovered that many people in the business were free with their advice, but I also found out that if I had tried to follow all of it I would have lost my sanity.

Be yourself, I was told. You fidget too much, I was warned. Don't let them change you, I was advised.

Smile more.
Don't smile without a reason.
Work to the camera.
Don't stare into the camera.
You talk too fast.
Be yourself.
Don't listen to anybody, do what you feel is right.

Don't worry about the cameras, make them find you.
Be sure you watch the red light so you know which camera is on.
Don't use cue cards.
Don't look down at notes.
Relax more.
Be yourself.
Don't scratch your nose, it looks awful.
You use your hands too much.
Sit still.
Don't let them change you.
Avoid profile shots.
Relax.
Be yourself.
Don't listen to anybody.

Very little of this advice came from Casey. He was, as I said earlier, primarily interested in the musical portions of the show. The fact that Betty Jean Ferguson was his wife may have had nothing to do with her being on the show (she was, in truth, quite a capable and attractive singer) but it was only normal that he should take considerable care in rehearsing and directing her songs. Then, there was Roy Roberts, possessor of a fine voice, whose songs also required rehearsal. And, of course, there was the orchestra, which had to sound just right. When and if there was time, we ran through the comedy sketches or blackouts that had been planned. And, naturally, if the show was too long, the simplest thing to do was to cut down the length of anything I was supposed to say. None of it mattered very much, anyhow, as long as the music came out all right.

Only two or three weeks after the show started, Casey complained to me about my "little jokes." His wife, who was then doubling as the band vocalist at the Royal York Hotel, had told him that some of the musicians had commented that they didn't think much of what I said was funny. I told him I wasn't quite prepared to accept every dance band musician in town as an authority on humor, but this made little impression on him. In his view, I was the "host" of the show. That word, in CBC usage, at least, is a kind of euphemism for announcer. Nothing more is really wanted—not a suggestion of individuality or personality or viewpoint.

Perhaps not all CBC officialdom felt this way, but enough of it did so that the attitude had filtered down to Casey; I'm sure he didn't originate the idea.

After four or five weeks, Len Casey surprised me with the news that he was being taken off the show. He could offer no explanation, because none had been given him.

I made some inquiries of my own about Casey's impending departure and found out the reason: he was to be replaced by Norman Jewison. The indication was that the CBC had plans for continuing the show beyond its summer commitment and it was considered worthy of Jewison's talents. (I'm not being snide; Jewison was then one of the CBC's top variety producers, Casey was relatively new to the field.) Until then, I didn't know Jewison very well, but I knew his work. He had done shows with Peppiatt and Aylesworth, Wally Koster, Denny Vaughan, Phyllis Marshall, Cal Jackson and others.

Jewison had been away on vacation and hadn't seen my show. But he telephoned me and we had a meeting one night, a week before he was to join the program. After talking to him, I couldn't help but feel pleased that he was coming in. It wasn't so much that I had any grievance against Casey, but simply that Norman and I hit it off, we were on the same wave length. In time, I also learned that he had a knack for building the confidence of performers, making them feel somewhat more important in the scheme of things than, say, a stagehand. This knack, I might add, was and is all too rare in television.

Jewison finished the rest of the summer season with us, some six or seven shows. Only Casey had left, the cast remained the same, but some of them were a little intimidated by Jewison. Expecting to be resented, he came on strong and made it abundantly clear that he was in charge. Not everybody liked it, but I did. Any producer who is replaced on a program is bound to feel hurt, and Casey was no exception. It must also have been difficult for Betty Jean to continue on the show with a producer whose presence she could hardly cheer under the circumstances.

But during those remaining weeks, Jewison took hold of the show and tried to strengthen it according to his own tastes and judgment. Since I liked doing interviews, some of these were arranged with people like Paddy Conklin, the exhibition midway impresario, and visiting film director Otto Preminger. One other change that worked out quite well was the addition of Jack Duffy. Jack was both a good singer and a natural comic. After some years of touring with musical groups, he had returned to Toronto and worked for a time on the Billy O'Connor Show. For our program, a character was created for him. Duffy became the "copy boy," the impish, irreverent character who was to get in my hair. Since I was identified as a newspaper columnist, the idea of a copy boy seemed to fit. It proved successful enough the first time it was tried so that Duffy became a regular on the show, appearing as the copy boy and also as a singer and sketch player. Jack was a strong asset to the show and he and I worked together many times, in those days and since.

Basically, what Jewison brought to the show (besides his acknowledged gifts as a director) was his willingness to have the show centred on me, to use me as something more than a "host." He encouraged me to have views and to express them on the show. We didn't always agree. At times, we argued heatedly—over a piece of material written for the show, over my involvement in a production, over the value of this guest or that—but at least I felt free to argue with him, I knew that he listened. He didn't simply impose his will on me, or "pull rank." He tried to persuade me, and sometimes he succeeded. Most important of all, we respected each other's views.

At the end of the summer series, the CBC decided to continue the show. It would be moved to Saturday nights (following the hockey telecast) but be on only every other week, alternating with Wayne and Shuster. Jewison rebuilt the show for this fall-winter season. Jack Duffy remained, as did Roy Roberts. But in place of Betty Jean Ferguson, he chose Gloria Lambert, a short, dynamic girl with a Judy Garland-type voice, from Massachusetts, who had been doing some television work in Montreal. Bill Isbister was succeeded as musical director by Gordon Kushner, and Phil Nimmons was hired to write musical arrangements. In addition, the Cynthia Barrett Trio was signed. Choreographed by Cynthia, the trio (Sally Dory, Lorraine Thomson and Andy Body) appeared regularly and always performed capably.

The author trying to look simultaneously thoughtful and photogenic for a CBC publicity picture.

Actor Larry Mann and producer-director Norman Jewison in a "Barris Beat" huddle. Below, the author and three cherished prizes, two from "Liberty" magazine for TV programs, the third—Mrs. Barris.

For comedy, besides Duffy, there was Sammy Sales and, frequently, Larry Mann. Also available was Bernie Orenstein, who, along with Sales, had joined me in writing the scripts. (Paul Hanover and Stan Daniels also wrote with us, for varying periods of time.) Sheila Billing became our billboard girl, later being succeeded by Babs Christie. And announcer Bruce Marsh became an integral part of the show. As guests, besides visiting performers, we had good jazz musicians like Moe Koffman, Oscar Peterson and Norman Amadio, plus offbeat interviews with tea leaf readers, hurdy-gurdy men, commercial jingle king Maurice Rapkin and others. We tried, as best we could, to avoid falling into a format rut.

Jewison's talent as a director was ever a delight. He had a flair for communicating to performers precisely what he wanted; when it became necessary, he could demonstrate any movement, gesture, facial expression, mood or delivery of a line. Although he had once been a performer (appearing in a couple of early editions of Spring Thaw) he was not comfortable before an audience, but in rehearsal he could uninhibitedly show any performer or actor just how he wanted something done. He had, in addition, infinite patience with performers once he felt they were trying to give their best. As a producer, he was equally impressive. He had (and still has) a charm about him, an ability to "sell" an idea to almost anyone, a cockiness in his manner that covered up whatever doubts he might be feeling. Our nickname for him was "Sammy Big," because he was slight of build but big in his manner and in his thinking.

(I have a vivid recollection of an evening, a few years later, when Jewison regaled a group of us at a Lake Simcoe summer cottage with the details of a story he had hopes of turning into a film. It was about a submarine full of Russians landing off the New England coast and the frantic attempts of the natives to mobilize their defenses. In his lengthy and hilarious recitation, Jewison acted out every part, ad-libbing the lines but getting across the style and manner of each character. None of us in that room had any doubts that he'd be able to sell the idea. He did, of course, and the result was the phenomenally successful "The Russians Are Coming.")

During that 1956/57 season, we had our ups and downs.

the cahh," New York came out New "Yawk" and, inevitably, fork came out "fawk." When, accidentally, Gloria inverted the order of the words in her line, it came out: "Use your fawk-n knife." We broke up in the studio, then panic set in, in anticipation of a great public outcry at what sounded like gross profanity. But not one single letter made reference to it. A cynic might argue that absolutely nobody was watching the program, but the facts indicate otherwise. While ours may not have been the most popular program on Canadian television, it did achieve some measure of success.

There have never been in this country any television awards equivalent to the Emmys in the United States. The closest thing we had—and they were sometimes subject to criticism—were the annual awards presented by the magazine, *Liberty*, in which television critics and columnists voted for their favorite Canadian programs and performers. For what it's worth, The Barris Beat did rather well in the 1956/57 season. It was named the Best New Show, and I was chosen as the Best New Performer and Best Master of Ceremonies.

Another, and possibly better, way of assessing the show's merit would be to indicate the calibre of some of the people who were involved in it, in terms of the later proof of their talents.

Norman Jewison hardly needs a boost here. After working in U.S. television with such stars as Harry Belafonte, Judy Garland, Jackie Gleason and Danny Kaye, he went into film directing. His credits include *In the Heat of the Night* (1967 Oscar winner as the best picture of that year), *The Russians Are Coming* (nominated for the same award the previous year), *The Cincinnati Kid*, *The Thomas Crown Affair* and *Gaily, Gaily*.

Our studio director during that 1956/57 season was Bernard Rothman, who has since written television shows for Danny Kaye, Judy Garland and other big stars.

Some of our other writers during the two-year life of The Barris Beat were: Bernie Orenstein, later writer of the Hollywood Palace and producer of the Phyllis Diller Show. Saul Ilson, writer-producer of The King Family, later producer of the Smothers Brothers Show. Allan Manings, who has written for Jackie Gleason, Red Buttons and other comics,

For comedy, besides Duffy, there was Sammy Sales and, frequently, Larry Mann. Also available was Bernie Orenstein, who, along with Sales, had joined me in writing the scripts. (Paul Hanover and Stan Daniels also wrote with us, for varying periods of time.) Sheila Billing became our billboard girl, later being succeeded by Babs Christie. And announcer Bruce Marsh became an integral part of the show. As guests, besides visiting performers, we had good jazz musicians like Moe Koffman, Oscar Peterson and Norman Amadio, plus offbeat interviews with tea leaf readers, hurdy-gurdy men, commercial jingle king Maurice Rapkin and others. We tried, as best we could, to avoid falling into a format rut.

Jewison's talent as a director was ever a delight. He had a flair for communicating to performers precisely what he wanted; when it became necessary, he could demonstrate any movement, gesture, facial expression, mood or delivery of a line. Although he had once been a performer (appearing in a couple of early editions of Spring Thaw) he was not comfortable before an audience, but in rehearsal he could uninhibitedly show any performer or actor just how he wanted something done. He had, in addition, infinite patience with performers once he felt they were trying to give their best. As a producer, he was equally impressive. He had (and still has) a charm about him, an ability to "sell" an idea to almost anyone, a cockiness in his manner that covered up whatever doubts he might be feeling. Our nickname for him was "Sammy Big," because he was slight of build but big in his manner and in his thinking.

(I have a vivid recollection of an evening, a few years later, when Jewison regaled a group of us at a Lake Simcoe summer cottage with the details of a story he had hopes of turning into a film. It was about a submarine full of Russians landing off the New England coast and the frantic attempts of the natives to mobilize their defenses. In his lengthy and hilarious recitation, Jewison acted out every part, ad-libbing the lines but getting across the style and manner of each character. None of us in that room had any doubts that he'd be able to sell the idea. He did, of course, and the result was the phenomenally successful "The Russians Are Coming.")

During that 1956/57 season, we had our ups and downs.

One of the more ridiculous incidents is probably remembered now only by me and, perhaps, a few early TV viewers in Prince Albert, Saskatchewan.

I received a call one day from Sydney Banks, an old friend of mine who was then with the S. W. Caldwell Company. He asked me if I would come to a film studio to appear in a one-minute promotional announcement about our show to be used by a new station in Prince Albert which was just joining the CBC network (as a privately owned affiliate) and would be carrying The Barris Beat. I gladly agreed and the small film chore was done on a Sunday afternoon. Then it occurred to me that I didn't know the call letters of the new station. I asked Banks, but he wasn't sure of them. I felt I should know, so that I could acknowledge their presence on our show the following week. I inquired at the CBC but was told there must have been some mistake—they knew of no new station being added to the network, in Prince Albert or anywhere else. What with meetings and rehearsals in the weeks following, plus the confusion over the existence of the new station, I forgot the whole matter.

A few weeks later, we received a telegram from the Prince Albert station informing us, in a rather injured tone, that they had been carrying The Barris Beat for several weeks and were still waiting for some on-the-air acknowledgment of their presence.

I was annoyed enough so that on the following program I related the whole incident and apologized to the Prince Albert station. Then I added that if there were any other stations receiving our show we'd appreciate hearing from them so we could inform the CBC, which didn't seem to be aware of who was or wasn't taking the show. The following Monday, Jewison was called on the carpet. The brass was incensed over my "indiscretion" and there was talk of pulling the program if I didn't behave myself. Norman managed to smooth things over, for the time being at least.

Another incident demonstrated to me how delicate are the feelings of television viewers. On one program, Oscar Peterson was a guest. Immediately prior to his appearance, we did some little comedy sketch or blackout that involved food. At the end of the sketch, I was to walk over to Oscar's piano, sit down beside him on the bench and chat with him.

On an impulse, I grabbed a sandwich from the table used in the sketch and when I got to the piano I offered Oscar half. We sat there for a few minutes, munching half a sandwich each and talking.

The following week, I received a disturbing letter from a man who said he used to enjoy our program—until now. But he felt I set a terrible example for all young Jews by munching a sandwich on a program during the high Jewish holiday, when fasting is required. The man was perfectly correct, of course, except for one vital point: he had mistakenly assumed I was Jewish. I had the unpleasant task, thus, of defending myself in a letter to this viewer without hurting his feelings or embarrassing him further.

This incident, plus others involving communiques from the public, helped to convince me of a truth about television to which I still cling: you can go on television and utter any five words in the English language—even something as bland as "good evening ladies and gentlemen"—and somewhere in this vast country someone will be offended. The public, I have found, is as willing as are those around you in television to give you advice about something you are supposedly doing wrong: you talk too fast, don't fidget, why didn't you ask so-and-so such-and-such a question, or why *did* you, you're too aggressive, you're too mild, you failed to mention Robbie Burns Day, you ignored the Ukrainian Christmas, you shouldn't have had "that woman" on you program. Everyone in television is subjected to this, of course. The pity of it is that too often too many of us tend to take this criticism too seriously. The result can be bland, colorless programs calculated to reach the ignoble goal of offending nobody.

Paradoxically, some things happen accidentally in television that you think will bring violent reactions—and nobody notices. On one of the Barris Beat shows, we had a sketch in which Jack Duffy, as a hunted criminal, returns home to a mother who forces food on him. Duffy was then supposed to tear into the food with his hands and Mama (played by Gloria Lambert) would admonish him to use his knife and fork.

As I have mentioned, Gloria was from Massachusetts and her speech habits reflected this. "Park the car" became "pahk the cahh," New York came out New "Yawk" and, inevitably, fork came out "fawk." When, accidentally, Gloria inverted the order of the words in her line, it came out: "Use your fawk-n knife." We broke up in the studio, then panic set in, in anticipation of a great public outcry at what sounded like gross profanity. But not one single letter made reference to it. A cynic might argue that absolutely nobody was watching the program, but the facts indicate otherwise. While ours may not have been the most popular program on Canadian television, it did achieve some measure of success.

There have never been in this country any television awards equivalent to the Emmys in the United States. The closest thing we had—and they were sometimes subject to criticism—were the annual awards presented by the magazine, *Liberty*, in which television critics and columnists voted for their favorite Canadian programs and performers. For what it's worth, The Barris Beat did rather well in the 1956/57 season. It was named the Best New Show, and I was chosen as the Best New Performer and Best Master of Ceremonies.

Another, and possibly better, way of assessing the show's merit would be to indicate the calibre of some of the people who were involved in it, in terms of the later proof of their talents.

Norman Jewison hardly needs a boost here. After working in U.S. television with such stars as Harry Belafonte, Judy Garland, Jackie Gleason and Danny Kaye, he went into film directing. His credits include *In the Heat of the Night* (1967 Oscar winner as the best picture of that year), *The Russians Are Coming* (nominated for the same award the previous year), *The Cincinnati Kid*, *The Thomas Crown Affair* and *Gaily, Gaily*.

Our studio director during that 1956/57 season was Bernard Rothman, who has since written television shows for Danny Kaye, Judy Garland and other big stars.

Some of our other writers during the two-year life of The Barris Beat were: Bernie Orenstein, later writer of the Hollywood Palace and producer of the Phyllis Diller Show. Saul Ilson, writer-producer of The King Family, later producer of the Smothers Brothers Show. Allan Manings, who has written for Jackie Gleason, Red Buttons and other comics, and later became one of the writers for the very successful Rowan and Martin's Laugh-In. Frank Peppiatt, who, with his partner, John Aylesworth, has written countless top variety shows on U.S. television. More recently, they produced the Jonathan Winters Show.

And then there was a young Englishman who was given a short-term contract by the CBC and assigned to us for a few weeks. He later vanished and nobody ever heard of him again until the opening of the first Beatles' movie, *A Hard Day's Night,* which he directed. His name was Richard Lester and he has since directed *A Funny Thing Happened On the Way to the Forum, How I Won the War,* and *Petulia.*

Whatever we may have thought of the show, however, rumors began to filter through to us toward the end of the season that our show was to be dropped. The rumors turned out to be true. I spent that summer as a panelist on a new program, Front Page Challenge. At the end of the summer, Harvey Hart, the producer of that program, told me he didn't think I was "right" for the panel but wanted me to "try out" as moderator, succeeding Win Barron. Then, it developed that Fred Davis was also to be tried, each of us doing the show for a few weeks, after which a final choice would be made.

At this point, I was invited to go to England with Jack Duffy to do four or six programs for Granada-TV. The invitation came from Stuart Griffiths, who had been with the CBC before going to England the year before. This was a tough decision to make. I did not relish the idea of being separated from my family for a couple of months, nor did I like the thought of uprooting my children and moving to England for what might be a short stay. I decided against going. Ironically, the day after I telephoned Griffiths to turn down his offer I received word from the CBC that Fred Davis had been chosen as the permanent moderator on Front Page Challenge. It was a disappointment, of course, but I still had my newspaper column, which could keep me busy enough.

Norman Jewison, meanwhile, was given a new assignment at the CBC that fall. He was to produce and direct Showtime and give it a "new look." At that time, Bob Goulet was still on that show. Jewison decided to move some of the Barris Beat people over: Gloria Lambert, Jack Duffy and arranger

Phil Nimmons. But somehow the mixture didn't seem to work and the sponsors (Canadian General Electric) weren't happy with the results. The CBC, responding to the sponsor's wishes, took Jewison off the show. The man they chose to replace him was Len Casey. I suppose it was only human that Casey should feel vindicated now that he was replacing a man who had replaced him on my show. In any case, Len was quoted in one newspaper story as saying he had been called in to "save the show" from the low state to which Jewison had plunged it.

However inept the sponsor may have considered Jewison, less than a year later, in New York, the same Jewison was chosen to direct a huge TV "Special" budgeted at the then astronomical figure of half a million dollars—a special observing the fiftieth anniversary of General Electric, who were sponsoring it. Before moving out of Canada, however, Jewison had one more crack at getting The Barris Beat back on the air—and succeeded. At his urging, the CBC decided to put the program on once more, again in a Saturday night spot but this time extended to an hour.

And so, in January, 1958, we were back again, with only a few changes in personnel. Gloria and Jack were still with us, although Jack decided he had had enough of the copy boy image and wanted to kill it. (In its place, we built up Bruce Marsh's part as the man who always picked on me.) Phil Nimmons now had his superb nine-piece jazz group on the show. Larry Mann and Sammy Sales were regulars, as was Maggie St. Clair, who did both comedy and musical numbers with Gloria and Jack.

The hour format was a welcome change for me. Now we had more time for interviews, for informal by-play, for the sort of anything-can-happen atmosphere that had first captured my interest on the Steve Allen show of several years before. But, inevitably, there were other problems. The kind of show I wanted to do, the direction in which we were now beginning to move, offered less of a challenge to a director of Jewison's calibre. Directing that sort of late night informal program is a thankless task. In the trade, such a director is referred to as a "picture taker."

Jewison had far too much creative ability and drive to be content with this, although it's to his credit that he always did his best to make the program succeed. During its two years, he managed to inject into it wherever possible some truly admirable directorial touches. His presentation of musical numbers was frequently stunning. His ability to extract from performers their very best effort was another valuable asset. Nevertheless, Jewison's talent needed more challenging scope. His departure for the United States was inevitable. He had gone as far as one can go in Canadian television; that he was capable of going much farther elsewhere has been amply demonstrated.

I'm not suggesting, incidentally, that The Barris Beat went off the air because Jewison left. True, he might have kept it going another season, or managed to get a bigger budget for it. But the program went off simply because it had run its course, in the view of the CBC. I'm not bitter about this, nor have I ever been. To get any program on the air requires faith in the program's potential on the part of someone in a key position. To take a program off the air does not require the enmity or vindictiveness of anyone—merely the absence of faith in its future by someone in a key position. That, apparently, is what happened to our show.

It happens, sooner or later, to most shows. Every time a new program goes on, an old one goes off. That's the nature of the business of television and it would be childish for anyone involved in the medium to seek for more sinister motives. One can argue, as I propose to in another chapter, that the CBC sometimes fails to give a program the kind of support and faith it needs at the outset. But that argument applies not merely to my show, but to many. It has to do with the CBC's philosophy (or lack of one) about the people in this country who appear on its television programs.

In any case, we had a two-year run with The Barris Beat. I had earned some extra money and my name was far more widely known than it had been before. I still wrote a newspaper column (for the *Telegram* now, instead of the *Globe and Mail*) and I had learned a fair bit about what goes on in a television studio. Besides all of that, a couple of weeks after the demise of The Barris Beat, I began work as moderator of a new CBC television show which was to run for fifty-six weeks.

But that's another chapter.

Panelists and Panic

Bernard Slade is an English-born Canadian now living in Hollywood, where he has had a hand in the creation of such television series as Bewitched, Living Doll, Love On A Rooftop and The Flying Nun. At Screen Gems, he is regarded as something of a genius and paid upwards of seventy-five thousand dollars a year.

After Bewitched and Living Doll, Slade felt he'd had his fill of gimmicky situation comedy shows, having helped create a television witch and a well-stacked female robot. But, Hollywood being a place where nothing succeeds like excess, Screen Gems were after him to dream up another such series. The way Bernie tells it, he took note of the fact that two of the most lucrative movies in years had been *Mary Poppins* and *The Sound of Music*. Since one involved a nanny who could fly and the other a lovable nun, Bernie decided the ideal show would simply combine the more successful characteristics of the two. The result was The Flying Nun, which Slade insists he submitted to the Screen Gems producers half in jest. Naturally, they loved it and the series became another smash hit. Slade shakes his head, more in bewilderment than sorrow, and enjoys the royalties.

Before he took the big plunge—moving to Hollywood—Bernie Slade had got his feet good and wet in Canadian television, after a fling at running a near-bankrupt summer theatre. In the 1950s and early 1960s he wrote several comedy scripts for television (and at least one very good serious one) and also was a regular writer for Cross Canada Hit Parade. The income from the latter made it possible for him to pursue the former.

In 1958 he submitted to the CBC an idea for a panel

show, which was accepted and produced under the title, "One Of A Kind." During its lifetime, Slade was the show's writer. It was a simple enough format. A panel of four persons would be asked to identify such "unique" and varied objects as Mickey Mantle's bat, Sally Rand's fan, Alexander Graham Bell's telephone or Sherlock Holmes's deerstalker cap. A guest—usually a well-known one—would represent the item and, after the guessing game was over, the guest would be interviewed by the panel.

Panel shows were then all the rage on American television, but the only one on CBC was Front Page Challenge, and so the Corp. decided it was time to put on another one, somewhat lighter in nature. The usual procedure in casting such a show is to hold "open auditions," meaning that any member of ACTRA (the Association of Canadian Television and Radio Artists, the performers' and writers' union here) is entitled to a tryout if he wants one. As well, the producers can also audition nonmembers, but no final decisions are made until everyone entitled to an audition gets his chance. This takes time, of course, and sometimes wastes time, but it is one way the CBC has of keeping peace with the union. I can't recall now just how many people were auditioned for One Of A Kind, but it must have been close to one hundred.

The panelists finally chosen were actor Lloyd Bochner, actress Kathie McNeil, and writers Rita Greer Allen and Allan Manings. It was, I think, a well-balanced panel for such a show. Lloyd had a considerable reputation as an actor and also happened to be an intelligent and articulate man. Kathie was attractive and animated, if not profound. Rita was knowledgeable and dignified. Allan's irreverent wit added some bite to the show. I was chosen as "host and moderator," as they say on television. As it happened, the producer was the same Harvey Hart who, a year before, had decided he didn't like me on the Front Page Challenge panel, then suggested my trying out as moderator on that show, and finally decided in favor of Fred Davis. But apparently he felt that I was right for One Of A Kind, a less serious show.

The program began as a summer replacement (often and logically the testing ground for new shows) and was continued through the following season. It did not get good notices from the TV critics, but that was hardly a surprise.

Critics tend not to like panel or game shows; only the public does. One of the Toronto weekly rags, which thrive on gossip and scandal, tried periodically to convince its readers that our show was "fixed." Although that sort of thing is usually irritating, I eventually learned there is no sense answering such charges. That kind of paper cares nothing for truth, only spicy items to brighten the dreary lives of its slack-jawed subscribers.

This was the time of the big quiz show scandals in U.S. television, of course, so it was probably inevitable that some people would view with suspicion any show that claimed honesty and spontaneity. But a small amount of common sense would have shown how ridiculous was the suggestion of fixing our kind of show. In the case of the American quiz programs, such as The Sixty-four Thousand Dollar Question and Twenty One, considerable sums of prize money were involved and evidently the "showmanship" of those running the shows led them to the stupid conclusion that giving contestants the answers before the show would assure happier results. It worked until word leaked out and the scandal followed.

On a game-panel show like ours, however, no such money was at stake. A viewer who sent in a suggestion was paid twenty-five dollars or fifty dollars. Those who had to guess the various mysteries were not "civilian" contestants, but professional performers who were paid a regular fee as panelists. They were chosen not particularly for their ability to ask probing questions in a guessing game, but for their charm, wit, personality and appearance. It couldn't have mattered less whether the panel guessed right or was stumped. What could possibly be gained by fixing such a show, even if anyone connected with it were tempted? The fun of a spontaneous show far outweighed any theoretical advantage in having a seemingly brilliant panel.

In any case, the show gave Canadian viewers the opportunity to see and hear from such diverse celebrities as Sir Cedric Hardwicke, Yousuf Karsh, Mitch Miller, Celia Franca, Gypsy Rose Lee, Jan Peerce, Celeste Holm and many more. This show, too, was done live, in those days before videotape, and the nature of it allowed for a certain amount of unpredictability. But that, too, was part of the fun.

I recall, for example, the visit of Xavier Cugat. The veteran Latin-American band leader brought along his dog, a frisky chihuahua, which he placed on the desk in front of him as he sat down next to me. As a regular practice, we had a pitcher of water and a glass on the desk in case a guest felt thirsty during the show. Cugat didn't need the water, but his dog did. In fact, throughout the interview the chihuahua kept lapping up water and I watched with growing uneasiness as I began to wonder how long it would take so much water to go through such a small dog. But we managed to get off the air with a dry desk.

Another, more harrowing incident involved a runaway bird and a secret drinker. At that time, one of the big U.S. programs was the weekly Perry Como Show. An incidental feature of that show was a beautiful white cockatoo named Snowflake. We invited the woman who owned Snowflake to bring the bird to Toronto for our show, thus confronting the panel with the monumental task of guessing "Perry Como's Snowflake."

The set in our studio (the Pierce-Arrow Showroom, of course) had two desks facing each other across the studio—one for the panel, one for me and the guests. But there was also a miniature stage, complete with curtains, which we sometimes used for displaying objects or, on occasion, for interviewing guests. In this case, we placed the woman with her bird on that stage. After the guessing game, I went to the stage to chat with the bird's owner. At the conclusion of this, the curtains were to close and we had a one minute break for a commercial before introducing the next guest.

The next guest was Frank Fay, a veteran actor and vaudevillian whose career included, back in the 1940s, a highly successful Broadway appearance in *Harvey*, the comedy about a man who owned an imaginary six-foot rabbit. Fay had a reputation as a heavy drinker, but when he arrived in Toronto that afternoon he volunteered the information that he hadn't taken a drink in years. As the day wore on, evidence to the contrary kept piling up, Mr. Fay having provided himself with a bottle of something which he stashed in his dressing room. By showtime, his protestations of sobriety became less and less intelligible.

Nevertheless, at the appointed time he took his place next

to me and a technician placed a neck microphone around his neck, all during the one-minute commercial following the interview with Snowflake's owner. However, as the curtains had closed, Snowflake got excited and began to fly around the studio. As we came back on the air, the panelists were mystified by the audience laughter. As was our custom, the panelists had put on blindfolds before the next guest, a recognizable celebrity, was ushered in. They knew nothing of the unannounced flight of the cockatoo.

Mr. Fay, deep in his alcoholic haze, spotted Snowflake and decided he would catch the bird. Unfortunately, he forgot he was noosed by a neck microphone and he damn near strangled himself, on the air. Then, Snowflake landed on my shoulder. Fay made a lunge for the cockatoo and I had visions of the poor (but highly valued) bird being mashed to death before the eyes of our horrified viewers. Fortunately, Snowflake must have got a whiff of Fay's breath, because he took off in time to escape the actor's clutches and flew straight back to his by now frantic owner.

On one show we had a real surprise guest—that is, we were surprised that we had him. The guest was Arthur Godfrey and the incident taught me that whenever possible it's much better to go to the top rather than deal with underlings. Our producer had tried in vain to lure Mr. Godfrey to our program. His agents, managers, hangers-on, network spokesmen and apologists all assured us that Godfrey was not available at any time under any circumstances.

Then Godfrey arrived in Toronto as a special attraction of the Royal Winter Fair. He was very proud of Goldie, his palomino, and couldn't resist any chance to ride the horse in public. Godfrey was to be in Toronto for a week, appearing nightly at the Winter Fair and broadcasting his daily radio show from his hotel. We had long since given up all hope of getting him to appear on One Of A Kind, because everyone concerned insisted he simply wouldn't have the time. When he arrived, on a Monday morning, I went to his press conference, in my capacity as an entertainment columnist for the *Telegram*. It was a pleasant morning conference, at which coffee was served. After the official conference was over, several of us stayed on to gab with him. Another newsman (I think it was Ray Timson of the Toronto *Star*) mentioned to Godfrey that I was host of a Canadian television panel show.

"Why can't I be on it?" Godfrey asked me.

I told him he was more than welcome but that we had been told he wouldn't be available. He asked me what night our show was on and what time we'd want him. I said it was Wednesdays and our show was on the air live from eight thirty to nine o'clock. "That's plenty of time. I don't go on at the Fair until later than that. I'll do it," he said. His assembled lackies didn't dare argue with him.

I was delighted, of course, but I'd learned to be cautious of that sort of casual commitment. I asked Godfrey who I should check with on the day of our show (two days hence) to see if he'd still be sure of being there. "You don't have to check with anyone," he said. "I said I'll be there, I'll *be* there."

Happily I reported all this to our producer, but we were all still uncertain as to how seriously we could take his word. We arranged to have a standby guest, who might or might not go on, depending on whether Godfrey got there. We had asked Godfrey to arrive about twenty minutes before air time, partly for make-up, but mostly to guard against his arriving late. On Wednesday night, at eight fifteen there was no sign of him. At eight twenty we were convinced he would not show up and told the standby guest he'd definitely be going on.

About three minutes before air time, Godfrey, resplendent in white tie and tails, followed by a phalanx of flunkies, and showing the effects of a long, luxurious dinner complete with abudant wines, sauntered into our studio and asked, "Where do you want me?"

He was, as it turned out, an excellent guest. His only complaint, when we ran out of time, was: "Is that all? Do I have to go now?" And out he went, surrounded by his obedient retinue, off to the Royal Winter Fair to mount his golden steed and ride gracefully towards the applauding crowd. Of all the guests we had on One Of A Kind, Arthur Godfrey was the least expensive. He didn't even bother to sign a contract, so he was paid nothing.

(A couple of nights later, I took my wife out to dinner at the Pump Room of the Lord Simcoe Hotel, then a fairly posh spot. Godfrey and a few friends were at the table next to us. I stopped to say hello and introduced my wife, then we sat down to dine. A little while later, Godfrey sent a bottle of wine to our table. When we were leaving, I stopped to thank him and he said it was "a pleasure to see a man enjoying himself with his own wife." But I couldn't escape the feeling that he wasn't quite sure where he'd seen or met me before.)

Another hectic incident involved the appearance of one Virgil Earp, whose claim to fame was that he was the genuine nephew of Wyatt Earp, the famed marshall of the Old West who had become the subject of a TV series. Virgil had become famous, too, by appearing on The Sixty-four Thousand Dollar Question as an expert on western lore. When he arrived to do our show, we discovered Virgil was about eighty years old and very nearly deaf. He was accompanied by his daughter, who told us Virgil refused to use a hearing aid, so we'd just have to speak up.

It was our custom on One Of A Kind, as it is on many other game shows, to have a sort of rehearsal in the afternoon. The regular panel, of course, was not present. Instead, we had a panel of actors sitting in for them. The purpose of this was to accustom the guest (many of whom came from outside Canada and had never seen our show) with the format of the program, and also for us to get some idea of the personality of the guest and the topics on which he might be most interesting.

One of Bernie Slade's duties was to prepare a list of questions that might be asked of a particular guest. This list was used in the afternoon rehearsal, and later was given to the real panel. (I hasten to add, for any skeptics, that the questions were not given to the panel until *after* the guessing portion of the game was over.) The panelists might use the prepared questions or substitute their own; it was merely a precaution, in case the panelists were not familiar with a guest's background.

On the day Virgil Earp was with us, one of the afternoon panelists asked him, during rehearsal, if he knew much about the famous gunfight at the O.K. Corral, in which Wyatt Earp had taken part. It was a happy choice (as Slade had expected when he included the question on the list) for the old man knew the story in detail and spent some six or seven minutes relating it, in a rather fascinating recital. Slade made a note to make sure this question was used on the show. The producer agreed and it was decided to allow old Mr. Earp ample time for his reminiscing. We used three guests on each show, with the "name" guest in the last place, so this meant economizing on the time alloted for the first two guests so Earp wouldn't be rushed.

On the broadcast, after the panel had guessed (or was told) who the guest was, the list of questions was passed out to them during a commercial. Bernie Slade had put a check-mark next to the question about the O.K. Corral, so the panel would not fail to notice it. No sooner did I invite the panel's questions to Mr. Earp than Lloyd Bochner obligingly asked him: "Mr. Earp, I suppose you know all about the famous gunfight at the O.K. Corral?" Pleased by Lloyd's alertness, I settled back to listen again to the long and interesting story. But old Mr. Earp double-crossed us. Having told the yarn that afternoon, I guess he was a little tired of it.

"Oh, sure," he said in answer to Bochner. "I know all about that."

Then he clammed up and waited for another question. What followed was seven or eight agonizing minutes of the dullest interview on record—not helped at all by the need for repeating every question so Mr. Earp could hear it.

It wasn't every week, of course, that yielded such surprises for us as last-minute arrivals or errant cockatoos. Nevertheless, the parade of celebrities afforded contact with a great variety of well-known people, not all of them totally lovable. Gypsy Rose Lee was irresistibly hilarious; Rudy Vallee was ridiculously pompous; Hal March was a good story-teller; Ann Landers was a compulsive advice-giver; Cornelia Otis Skinner was completely charming; Burgess Meredith was thoroughly bored; Mitch Miller had both eyes on one of our pretty researchers; Kate Reid was too nervous to enjoy being on the program; Walter Susskind was urban; Allen Funt failed to charm any of us.

But equally rewarding was the regular contact with the people who were connected with the program. Bernie Slade was truly born to be a success in Hollywood. Not simply because he's bright and inventive, although we knew that.

But he has always taken easily to luxury and leisure, and those of us who knew him here had no doubt that he would one day enjoy living on the Hollywood scale. His equally delightful wife, actress Jill Foster, has always had that special talent for understanding her husband's idiosyncrasies and taking them in her stride. Lloyd Bochner, perhaps considered stiff and aloof by people who didn't know him very well, had a nice, dry wit that now and then took everyone by surprise. Lloyd has always been a gentleman and one thing he never appreciated was coarseness, particularly in women.

One time, he worked on a television program here with a Hollywood actress of French birth. She happened to be one of those women who like to shock people by being candid to the point of vulgarity. She also had some far-out theories which she loved to express. After the program was completed, Lloyd and some others joined the French actress at a nearby lounge for a drink or two. The actress promptly began expounding one of her pet theories: that all actors are homosexuals, that they have to be, it's part of their personality, and so on. She knew, incidentally, that Lloyd was an actor. As both an actor and a heterosexual, Lloyd was offended by this nonsense, but he saw no point in arguing with her. At one point in her dissertation, the lady turned to Lloyd to ask his opinion. Unable to remember his name, she said: "You—monsieur—what is your name, again?" Without batting an eye, Lloyd answered: "Gladys."

My favorite person on One Of A Kind was Allan Manings. I had known him before. Over the years, we have worked together on a number of projects, in television, radio and also in the theatre. When you get to know him, Manings is a sensitive, soft-hearted man of considerable intellectual capacity and a penchant for serious and usually antiestablishment causes, to which he commits himself wholeheartedly. But on the surface he is brash, quick-witted, irreverent, even pugnacious. He is as quick to praise as to condemn and is virtually incapable of hiding his emotions. When he argues, his bearded chin juts out accusingly.

On One Of A Kind, a guest one week was Basil Rathbone, the late British actor famous for his movie portrayals of Sherlock Holmes. In an attempt to disguise his voice (the panelists were blindfolded) he assumed a rather embarrassingly exaggerated Chinese accent, of the "no-tickee-no-shirtee" vintage. Manings, who has no tolerance for any sort of ethnic humor, could barely wait his turn to question the mystery guest. When it came he could hardly contain his scorn. "I assume," he said, "by that terrible accent that you are Bulgarian."

But Manings was at his best when he saw the humor in something around him, even if nobody else did. He could not resist comment and he would never sink to the level of adding afterwards, "I was only joking . . ." or "but seriously. . . ."

One evening he was dining alone at Julie's Restaurant, an elegant dining room located in what was once the Massey mansion in Toronto. While he was there, two young couples came in to dine. Conspicuously overdressed, they were obviously celebrating some special occasion. Midway through their meal, a waiter and a busboy collided near their table. As two laden trays flew into the air, salads, soups, sauces, vegetables and crockery cascaded down over the startled foursome at the table.

Horrified, Julie Fine, the owner, stepped in quickly and with the help of a few concerned employees tried to clean off the guests' fancy clothing. Somehow, the two couples were mollified and the meal was served again. It was, under the circumstances, on the house.

Manings, like everyone else in the room, had observed all this. When he was leaving, he walked past Julie Fine, who was still trying to get over the humiliating experience. He tapped Julie's shoulder and said: "Loved the jugglers."

Another nutty experience endeared me to Allan. At the close of a Barris Beat season, Norman Jewison and I decided to throw a joint party for all involved in the show. It was to be at my house, which had more room, and Jewison asked me to buy everything and then straighten out the costs with him later.

My wife and I planned the guest list and the refreshments, and one morning, a day or two before the party, I went off to the liquor store to stock up for the occasion. I had to stop off briefly at the CBC offices first and there ran into Manings. When I told him where I was going he offered to come along to help.

Picture it. This was a Monday morning. We arrived at the liquor store a few minutes before it was due to open at 10 A.M. The clerk who unlocked the huge glass doors must have had us figured as winos right away.

I went through the ridiculous Ontario ritual of making out purchase slips for all the liquor—something like eight bottles of rye, six of Scotch, four of gin, three of vodka, three of rum, and so on. I took the slips to the cashier, then went to the counter and placed the order with the clerk, the same dour fellow who had unlocked the doors.

It took him a while to fetch all the bottles and place them on the counter. Then he asked if I wanted them in boxes and I said that would be fine. All the time he was packing the liquor he kept glaring disapprovingly at Manings and me. Allan looked back at him blankly but didn't say a word. When the liquor was packed, I lifted one box and Manings took the other and we started out.

Just as we were halfway through the doors, Allan turned around—somehow he sensed the clerk was still staring at us —and, with a big grin on his face, said: "See you tomorrow."

My favorite Manings one-liner concerns a time when I took him with me, this time to a dinner party. We were working together that summer, writing a show called "Swing Gently." I had been invited to a cocktail party and dinner being given by Warner Brothers Pictures and, since my family were out of town, I invited him to come along with me. The party was in honour of Joseph E. Levine, the dynamic movie entrepreneur who was then making a small fortune by buying the world rights to a series of dreadful Hercules films made in Italy. He had recently completed an arrangement with Warner Brothers to distribute one of these turkeys and was in Toronto to promote the picture.

Warners decided on the dinner party for the press, of which I was still a member. It was a ludicrous affair, held in a hotel ballroom and calculated to exploit the Greek theme (?) of the Hercules film. Waitresses were draped in Grecian gowns, a combo of musicians looked ill at ease in togas and sandals, and wine was poured from earthenware decanters rescued from the props department of some De Millean epic. After an hour or so of drinking we were all—perhaps a hundred of us—urged to sit down to dinner. Since this was an "informal" party there was no head table. Round tables seating eight or ten were all about the room. In almost the exact centre was the round table at which Mr. Levine and the Warner Brothers dignitaries were seated. Allan and I were with a group at the next table.

As the dinner drew to a close, Al Dubin, the Warner Brothers publicist here, rose to his feet and discreetly tapped a spoon against the side of a water glass to gain the crowd's attention. He then introduced our "host" and we all settled back, resigned to paying for our meal by listening to a long-winded, long-playing commercial on the merits of the new Hercules film. Mr. Levine got to his feet amid polite, even restrained applause. His speech lasted no more than ten seconds. "I want to welcome everybody here," he said. "God bless you for coming." Then he sat down.

Everyone was so relieved that the applause following such unprecedented brevity was thunderous. But Manings was not a man to pass up such an opportunity. Just as the long applause died away, in that moment of silence before the chatter would begin again, Manings turned to me and, in a stage whisper that could be heard in a good part of the room, said: "Great speech, till he dragged religion into it."

It's this sort of flair for jumping at any opening for a debunking comment that makes Allan Manings both a stimulating companion and a successful writer. No doubt, it has had much to do with his success as one of the writers on Rowan and Martin's Laugh-In. Inasmuch as his personality reflected this irreverence, I always felt it made him a valuable television personality. (After One Of A Kind, Allan had a longer run on another CBC panel show, Flashback.)

For a time the CBC seemed content with One Of A Kind, but after a little over a year they decided to drop it. Bernie Slade has always maintained the show was killed because it was his own "property" rather than the CBC's and the Corporation was uneasy about running a show that it didn't own outright. Earlier, the CBC had experienced some ticklish dealings with John Aylesworth over the ownership of Front Page Challenge. An agreement was finally reached with him, but the CBC might well have been loath to get again involved in such a tricky situation. In any case, when One Of A Kind was taken off the air, it was immediately replaced by another and somewhat similar show called "Live A Borrowed Life." This one, however, "belonged" to the CBC. It ran for several years.

Just before One Of A Kind hit the dust, CBC producer Bob Jarvis asked me to write a summer series he was to produce titled "Swing Easy." The series, with Ruth Walker, the Rhythm Pals and Alan Millar, was a light summer variety show that marked my first assignment as a TV writer, apart from the writing I had done for The Barris Beat. But more than that, it marked the beginning of an association with Bob Jarvis which was to last, on and off, for a number of years. In the fall of that year (1959) he was assigned to take over production of the Juliette Show, and he asked me to become its writer.

The Queen

People in television often refer to Juliette as "the only star" in Canada. This is sometimes said admiringly, by her fans; sometimes derisively, by critics of the CBC's antistar system; sometimes grudgingly, by people who recognize her stature in an area where the Canadian public tends to be unenthusiastic.

Whether Juliette is indeed the "only" star is perhaps debatable. Certainly in terms of public recognition Wayne and Shuster are stars (known outside of Canada as well as in), and so are Tommy Hunter, Gordon Sinclair, Fred Davis and Don Messer. In her time here, Shirley Harmer was certainly popular, as was Bob Goulet. In sports, surely people like Bobby Hull, Frank Mahovlich and Nancy Greene have to be regarded as stars. But in a certain sense, Juliette is the only star. She is a star partly because she *believes* she is a star, she behaves like one, she has the bearing of a star, the glamour, the authority, the remoteness, even the temperament.

No one has ever seen Juliette looking other than her best. If she shops at the supermarket (and she isn't seen doing that too often) she is smartly dressed, flawlessly groomed. Her own clothes are often as expensive as those she wears on TV and frequently in better taste. She knows she is being observed and never lets any part of the public see her in anything but the kind of clothes a star is expected to wear. Where she goes her aura goes. Her famous smile is natural, but it shines a little brighter if there are people around watching her.

But being a star is not as difficult as becoming one. Here,

too, Juliette is unusual in Canada. She has the fierce determination, the dedication to work, the iron ego needed for stardom. Too many of Canada's entertainers—particularly the females, it seems to me—want stardom without sacrificing anything for it. They would like to be stars, preferably overnight, and only if it's convenient. They want the glamorous trappings of stardom, but they also want to get home in time to cook dinner.

But Juliette Sysak was never like that. In a country that has lamentably little opportunity for a singer or actor to "grow up in the business," Juliette grew up singing. Born in Winnipeg of Ukrainian parents, she was singing as a child. When the Sysaks moved to Vancouver Julie continued singing. By the time she was a teenager she was known on radio; later she worked as a band vocalist. She was a child when Shirley Temple was the rage; she was a pretty blonde singer when Alice Faye was a star; she was a popular Vancouver entertainer when Betty Grable was everybody's favorite pinup.

Although she was fairly well known in the West, Canada as a whole first became aware of Juliette as the rather beefy, jolly singer on the Billy O'Connor show on Saturday nights. O'Connor, a glib, gravel-voiced Irish leprechaun, helped build an audience for Julie and lived to regret it. After a couple of years, the sponsors (and the CBC) sensed a public preference for Juliette and she inherited the Saturday night show. She and Billy O'Connor have rarely seen each other since.

The Juliette Show had already been on the air for three or four seasons when I was hired as its writer. Julie was apprehensive. Not only was she getting a new producer, Bob Jarvis, who had the reputation of being rather wild, but a new writer she hardly knew. I didn't know her well enough to realize it then, but what terrified Juliette most was change. Some time later I told her she was a true conservative, according to Mort Sahl's definition: "A true conservative is someone who believes nothing should be done for the first time." She laughed heartily and accepted the description.

Before Jarvis and I joined the program, the producer had been Syd Wayne and the writer Saul Ilson. When Wayne heard I was going to be the writer, he passed along a suggestion: "Saul never took a writing credit," he told me. "On this kind of show, it should seem as if Julie makes up her own lines and when the audience sees a writing credit, that illusion is destroyed." I thanked him for his suggestion but ignored it. Writing was my business and I had no intention of helping to perpetuate the myth that TV performers "make up" their own words.

But it really didn't matter. In those days, Juliette's attitude toward writers was about as naive as was the CBC's. The corporation barely tolerated writers as a kind of act of largesse. (Not long before, the CBC had embarked on a series of "spectaculars" for Chrysler, budgeted at seventy thousand dollars each. These variety hours were over-loaded with important artists, but significantly the CBC didn't think it important enough to assign a writer to the series.)

Juliette used to refer to me as the "continuity writer," a stale phrase left over from her radio days that bears very little relationship to the function of a writer in television variety. In any case, I soon learned that Julie often changed things into her own words, sometimes sounding more natural, but also sometimes losing the point intended in the script. After a while, I learned not to worry too much about it. In truth, the words Julie spoke didn't always matter too much. More than any other of Canada's female singers, she had (and has) a flair for seeming comfortable on camera. In addition to those personality traits I mentioned earlier, what made her a star was the ability to "front" a show, to carry its burden. She has presence, authority, a distinguishable personality.

When I first joined the show, it was that little twenty-minute program that everyone (including the CBC) took for granted. It operated on a shoestring budget and got by mostly on the loyalty of Julie's own following. Her own major complaint – and it was a deeply-rooted one that persists to this day—was that despite her success the CBC never quite appreciated her. She had to fight to get an increase in the budget for gowns, for a hairdresser, for anything that might improve the prestige of the show. And yet she was the CBC's biggest star.

But Jarvis was an energetic and resourceful producer. He

talked the CBC into expanding the show, the following year, into a full half hour and increasing its budget enough to dress the show up a little with some guests. At that time, the program had Juliette, a rather smallish band under pianist Bill Isbister, the vocal quartet called the Romeos and a weekly featured spot by trumpeter and novelty singer Bobby Gimby.

Almost from the beginning, I was aware of the coolness between Juliette and Gimby. I never did learn much about its root beyond a vague story that she was convinced (on what evidence, I don't know) that he was trying to take over the show, while he was equally certain (probably on no more concrete evidence) that she was trying to ease him out. They rarely spoke to each other except when it was necessary, and that meant usually only when they were on camera. (In fact, I rarely wrote anything that would use them together because I knew this only created problems.) Gimby regularly complained to Jarvis about her alleged offenses. She, being the queen, hardly deigned to take notice of him. I remember Bobby getting angry one week because she had introduced him, in rehearsal, as "Bob Gimby" rather than "Bobby." He went to Jarvis, charging that "she knows damn well I'm known as Bobby, but she does it deliberately." Jarvis cooled him down and diplomatically got Juliette to use Gimby's correct billing. But such incidents were frequent and the feud went on, with Jarvis often in the middle and me watching from the sidelines. The final blowup was inevitable, but when it came it was rather beautiful, too.

The Juliette program had other problems, however. To some extent these were Julie's own fault. Her greatest flaw was a lack of confidence in herself, curious though that may seem. Jarvis and I often discussed the artificial limitations she seemed to place on herself. Even when she was dimly aware that her style—her appeal—were behind the times she was afraid to try change. She would rarely sing a new song unless it was already a big hit. When I suggested "Never On Sunday," after I'd heard it for the first time, I was almost laughed out of the meeting. "I'm no pioneer," she argued when a new song was suggested. "Let Sinatra and Peggy Lee do that. I'll do songs the public knows."

She had a kind of image of herself that she was loath to tamper with. In fairness to her, this was understandable. For years she had sung "standard" songs in a standard way. She represented a kind of wholesome glamour, like a grown up Shirley Temple, with a dash of Betty Grable added. She had grown up (professionally) in an era when the big smile went with the big voice and the big finish to the song. She dressed beautifully, she laughed earthily and she spoke romantic banalities. To her public—the largely square Canadian public—she represented an ideal combination: just flirty enough to keep the husbands watching, but just "nice" enough not to be resented by the wives. She was a coquette, but not a seductress, Alice Faye rather than Rita Hayworth. (If the comparisons I'm picking seem dated, this is intentional—you wouldn't think of relating Julie to Marilyn Monroe or Barbra Streisand, for they had no part in shaping her style.) It's revealing that her TV public was dominated by older people, not young-marrieds or swingers.

Anyway, that image had always worked; it had taken her a long way, from a modest Ukrainian home in western Canada to television stardom. Thousands of her contemporaries could ask for no more. In a way, it still worked. She could charm audiences and ad agency men alike with the same throaty laugh, melodious voice and clean glamour that somehow let you know that all the saucy looks and romantic lyrics were really just in fun and deep down she was still a nice Ukrainian girl from western Canada.

She had come up the hard way and was proud of it. She had little formal professional training, a high school education and severely limited horizons beyond her own world of singing. If she was aware, deep inside herself, that she was getting by partly on bluff—and I believe she was—she saw no choice but to go on bluffing, smiling and exuding a confidence she only partly felt.

She worked hard, too, in her way. She was certainly serious about her work. She knew which songs were good for her, or, at least, "safe." She knew she had to preserve that glamorous image on TV and she made certain she did. In the studio she could always see a monitor, was always acutely aware of how she looked. She was demanding about lighting and camera angles—the image was all-important.

But she displayed no capacity for growth as an artist. She had no adventurous spirit, no desire to try something different, no urge to face a new challenge, no willingness to alter in any way that tried-and-true image. Anyone who suggested that any change was desirable was bound to be viewed with some hostility.

Jarvis tried, I tried. He was always more successful than I. After a time, she learned a cautious respect for him. She accepted him as an ally, rather than a reckless wild man bent on destroying her. Even so, he had to be persuasive, sometimes even devious. "Alex and I were kicking around an idea," he once said at the beginning of a meeting. "He didn't think you could do it, but I bet him you could." Sometimes this kind of oblique attack would work, but not always. As for me, I don't think she ever got over regarding me with some suspicion, some doubt. We got along well, generally, but any ideas I had for the program were usually passed on through Jarvis, not only because that was the usual chain of command, but because Julie was more inclined to trust his judgment than mine.

One thing that got in the way of change was Julie's fear of giving the public the wrong impression, whatever that was. She was profoundly respectable and determined to be considered so. One time, we conned her into doing a little satirical soap opera sketch in which she was the heroine and guest George Murray was the hero. It wasn't hilariously funny, but it was a change of pace.

All during rehearsals, Julie was giggly — a sure sign of nervousness about the material. She finally did the sketch and it came off fairly well, but then she spoiled it—for me, at least—by announcing to the audience that it had all been in fun and she had Tony's (her husband's) permission to do the romantic sketch with George Murray. She was actually worried lest some old biddy might seriously think she was "making love" to George.

Tony Cavazzi has been Juliette's husband since the Vancouver days. She often liked to mention him on the air, although he was rarely seen. He played (and still does) in the orchestra on all her shows. One reason their childless marriage has survived these many years, I think, is that Tony, a mild, soft-spoken man, is a genuine Juliette fan.

Hers is the career in the family and although, out of concern for his feelings, Julie sometimes makes a show of relying on Tony for guidance and advice, she really makes her own decisions in her work. He sometimes accompanies her to brass meetings when a contract is to be negotiated, but he never attended production meetings for the program. At rehearsals he was simply a member of the orchestra and never entered into any discussions concerning Julie's work on the show. Any talking they may have done about the program or her career must have been in private. In public, Julie and Tony always presented a picture of the happy marriage and I never heard or saw anything to suggest the contrary.

Before I joined the program, I had heard that Juliette was difficult to work with. This turned out to be only partly true. She could be difficult with people she didn't like or distrusted, but she could also be generous and loyal and considerate. The first time Marg Osborne (of the Don Messer Show) was a guest on the program, Juliette went to great lengths to make the Halifax singer feel at ease. "I know what it's like," she said, "coming to Toronto to do a show. You're scared stiff." Her own attitude had much to do with lessening Marg's sense of awe at being in Toronto and on the Juliette program.

She was loyal, also, to Bill Isbister, the musical director of the program, and he was loyal to her. Whether he really served her best interests is something else. Perhaps because his own outlook was as conventional as hers, he never corrected her or disagreed with her. At times, this bothered me. I felt he was the one person with a solid enough musical background to wield some influence over Julie, to guide her towards some expansion as an artist, to help her grow. But he never did. He went along, the safe, tried and true way. He never argued.

One show day, I became aware of something strange in the way she was singing a particular song. After listening several times, I realized Julie was singing it wrong. I went to Bill to check on it, rather than make a fool of myself. He hadn't noticed, he said. I urged him to check it. We got out the sheet music and, simply by playing it through, proved that Julie was, indeed, singing it wrong. "Oh, well," said

Bill, "it doesn't really matter. She's learned it that way now. Let it go." No, it didn't matter. That particular little error didn't really matter. What mattered was that no one was going to correct Julie, no one was going to suggest there was any possibility of improvement.

This sort of docility had its effect on the program. Gino Silvi, who did the choral arrangements and chose the Romeos' songs, was also a champion of the conventional. It became a wry gag on the show that his definition of a "good" arrangement was one that had been used before. It was appalling how often we repeated material, partly because it was "safe," partly because it was easier. Once, when Maggie St. Clair, the show's choreographer for a time, and I expressed criticism of Bill's lifeless, unimaginative arranging and conducting, Julie leaped to his defence and was horrified that we were trying to "knife" Isbister. (That it was intended for *her* benefit didn't even occur to her). Her hostility towards Maggie, in particular, never let up.

So it went. Julie's approach—sustained by some of those around her—was that she had only to give the public what it expected and wanted. At Christmas time, we did a Christmas show. We also did Easter shows, Thanksgiving shows, New Year's Eve shows, Remembrance Day shows and Mother's Day shows. From year to year, these hardly varied. I know—I still have the scripts on file. It was true, as Julie argued, that the public "expected" this of her. What she failed to perceive was that what excited the public, what snapped it out of its lethargy, was the unexpected. The same fickle public that wanted Juliette never to change, and for whom she doggedly refused to change, eventually got over the novelty, tired of her smile, her warmth, her sentimentality, her wholesome glamour.

The trouble with any weekly television show is that even if it's every bit as good the tenth year as it was the first, it won't seem as good. It has to run downhill; no public remains constant. Still, Juliette lasted for ten years and today she is still thought of as a star. One can't think of her in any other way. Nor can one work with Julie for four years and come away without feeling great respect and admiration for her, sometimes even affection.

She was and probably still is rather insecure. Perhaps this

has something to do with her background. She has that slightly unsure way of the non-Anglo-Saxon in a WASP society. Perhaps it has also to do with her insularity. Her world is bordered by spotlights, audiences, cameras and the make-up room. She is not interested in politics or sports, hobbies or horticulture, religion or art. When she goes to the theatre it's almost exclusively to musicals. Her newspaper reading is largely restricted to the entertainment pages. I never heard her discuss a book, except perhaps the biography of a show business personality. She is Canadian and proud of it (though I doubt she could articulate why) but she worships stars like Sinatra or Garland, of whatever nationality.

Show business is her business and she is absorbed in it. She and Tony usually go to Las Vegas in the summer to see night club shows, and occasionally to New York for the latest musicals. She is usually up on show business gossip and trade talk, though rarely susceptible to trends. She was always at her best while working. When she had a strong guest with her, she rose to the occasion and performed her best, in the manner of a real trouper. She liked working with Earl Wrightson, who had a big musical comedy voice and the courtly manners that titillated her. George Murray was another favorite, partly, I felt, because she identified with his tenacious struggle to carve out a continuing career. But there were others she didn't take to. Jerry Vale made her uncomfortable because he was too short; Jackie Davis was too hip. Generally, she liked women guests more than men—Marg Osborne, Eleanor Collins, Peggy Neville.

Like many performers, she was more confident during rehearsals than on a show, when the pressure becomes greater. On an actual show, that precious image was on the line. Doing a moderate rock-and-roll number with a group of singers, she Twisted quite adeptly in rehearsal—but she didn't have the guts to do it on the show. She often tossed in funny or irreverent (but not smutty) lines in rehearsals, but no one could persuade her to leave them in for the show. Someone might misunderstand.

Once, when Gordie Tapp was on the program, they did an uninhibited number in hobo outfits. Juliette really unbent and had fun with it. She was a revelation. But the explanation was simple, and even she admitted it. She was "being somebody else," not the glamorous, neatly dressed, impeccably coiffured Juliette — she could clown around without fear of criticism.

Being a woman, she was given to sudden changes of heart. At the beginning of one season, drummer Johnny Niosi joined the band and so high was her regard for his musicianship that her praise for him and her delight that he was on the show were boundless. But a few weeks later she listened to a playback of a program and noticed that the drums were too loud on one of her numbers. From then on, Johnny was referred to, rather tartly, as "that drummer."

Resistance to innovation was second nature. Once she had accepted Jarvis, she wanted no one else. Now and then, Bob would be removed for a week or two for some special and Julie would promptly get depressed. She was suspicious of anyone she didn't know, even suspected the CBC was doing it deliberately to undermine her.

On one such occasion, when another (less seasoned) producer was filling in for Jarvis, Juliette went so far as to turn to me for advice. In his absence, I guess I was the last resort. At rehearsals that week, she frequently asked me what I thought about this or that, and even though I was flattered I still winced when I realized that at the same time she was making it brutally clear—in front of cast and crew—that she had no faith at all in the substitute producer.

Her fear of the unfamiliar was almost fanatic. If she was invited to a banquet, she would have a snack before leaving home—just in case the dinner was something she didn't like. She loved Italian cooking and almost anything Italian (an interest she naturally acquired through Tony) but she kept delaying a proposed European trip because she was afraid she might not enjoy the food, the water or the climate. (She and Tony finally went and loved it.)

Julie's fear and mistrust of the press was perhaps more understandable, but still extreme. She never fared well with TV critics, whose tastes were often more sophisticated than those of the Saturday night Juliette audience. Some critics were unduly harsh; they knocked her for smiling, for giggling, for being old-fashioned, for lasting so long, for anything. It got to the point where Juliette preferred no coverage at all to the slightest criticism. Undoubtedly, her early cautiousness towards me had something to do with my newspaper background. At that time, I was still covering the entertainment scene for the *Telegram* in Toronto and although I had never been especially rough on her in print she lumped me with all press people, simply not to be trusted.

Once, while I was writing her TV show, I learned—not from her—that Julie was to be the New Year's Eve attraction at one of Toronto's big hotels. I had never seen her work in a club before and I expressed interest. She became flustered, asked if I was going to review her act and frankly told me she'd rather I didn't. In the end, I did go to see her, enjoyed it very much and said so in print. But that didn't change her mind about the press. But even regarding the press, she could be unpredictable. If she read a particularly brutal notice of some performer's work, she felt genuine sympathy for the artist. But if someone she didn't like received favorable notices, she complained that the press was never "honest."

She seemed to me uneasy around children. We occasionally used children on the show (on the Christmas show, for example, when the children of those associated with the program would be seen) and Julie would laugh nervously and joke about the "little monsters." But in an unguarded moment, she told one of the girls on the program that she deeply wished she had had children.

Like any star—or queen—she was at her best when she was the centre of attention. She enjoyed entertaining occasionally, at the immaculate Rosedale apartment she and Tony share. Sometimes she would hold a bigger party at a hotel banquet room for people who worked with her, and the end of a TV season usually meant another party with Juliette happily holding forth as gracious hostess. But she was also thoughtful (and wise) enough to look after her TV crews. After the last show of a season, she would supply cases of beer and fried chicken or pizza for everyone — camera crews, stagehands, lighting men and the rest.

Stories about Juliette abound. Most of them, I'd heard before I met her. She was supposed to be hard as nails, she was given to tantrums, she was foul-mouthed, she would never allow another blonde to appear on her program. As usual, the stories were just myths.

Yes, she could be tough, just tough enough to survive in a tricky, competitive business. But I have known a lot harder people than Juliette, in and out of show business. If she had tantrums, they must have been very private. There were times when the program wasn't going too well and she was edgy or impatient, hardly an abnormal reaction. But in four years I never saw anything like a trantrum. I never saw her stalk off a set, or refuse to work, or make unreasonable demands. She was sometimes unhappy about aspects of the show—usually having to do with her own appearance—but she didn't create scenes.

As for the ban on blondes, that too was unfounded. After all, how many blondes were there around who could qualify as guests? There was Joan Fairfax, who had her own program for a time; Sylvia Murphy, who had virtually retired from the business; Betty Robertson, who did appear with Juliette; and that's about it. In fact there were a few other blondes, of less stature, who did appear on Juliette's show. In any case, she was not afraid of competition, blonde or otherwise. If there were potential guests she was opposed to welcoming, her reasons—however emotional or illogical had nothing to do with hair (or skin) color.

When something or someone hurt her, she reacted normally—she became angry. For a few years after the split between Juliette and Billy O'Connor, they had no contact. Then Bob Jarvis thought it might be fun to have O'Connor as a guest on the show, as a sort of reunion. He suggested this to Julie and she agreed. That it never came to pass was as much Billy's fault as hers. Billy was then working in night clubs and, in his troupe, he had a new "discovery," an attractive singer whose talent impressed him. In his enthusiasm, he began introducing her to audiences as "the new Juliette" or "the girl who's going to knock Juliette out of Saturday night." Inevitably, word of this got back to Julie and she cooled to the idea of having O'Connor as a guest. Jarvis dropped the idea.

The matter of Juliette's language has also been exaggerated. To begin with, a certain amount of loose, flippant,

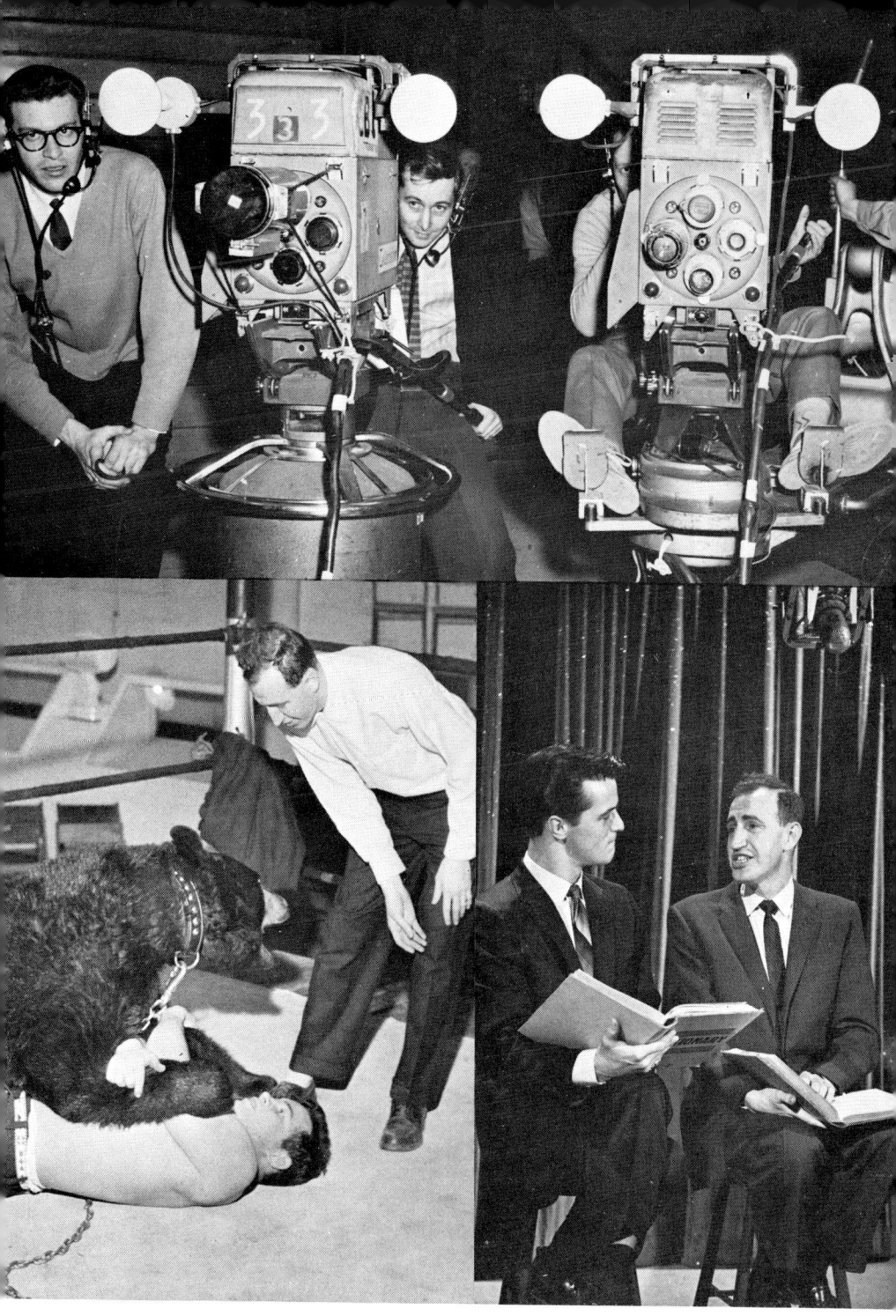

The view from the business end of TV cameras. Wrestling the bear is Dave McKinley, who later repeated the feat on our program. Barris and the bear did an apathetic waltz, but the bear insisted on leading. At lower right, an appearance with Robert Goulet on "Showtime."

Among the culprits in this scene from Jack Duffy's program are Alfie Scopp, George Raymond, Larry Mann and Billy Van. Below, Barris and Duffy flank Gloria Lambert in a number titled "Triplets."

At a Juliette rehearsal, with pianist Bill Isbister and producer Bob Jarvis. Below, panelist Allan Manings and guest Mitch Miller compare beards while the author's head blocks the name of the program.

Getting Arthur Godfrey to the studio was no easy task, but once there he proved an entertaining guest.

Newspaper want ads provided the basis for this production number on "In Person."

habitual profanity is pretty standard in show business. Julie's was no worse than many others'. In fact, it was probably a handy release for her—on camera, she was so consistently goody-goody that it must have been an unconscious kick to swear a bit off camera. She could take an off-color story, but rarely told any; she was no storyteller, anyway. In moments of anger or impatience, her language could get a bit salty, but not enough to raise a show business eyebrow.

She liked to joke about sex in a giddy, womanish way. But the more you got to know her the more you realized it was all talk. As a "glamorous" TV star, I guess she figured a superficial preoccupation with sex was expected of her, along with sly winks and the earthy laugh. But she was at heart an old-fashioned, moral, highly respectable girl, brought up in a good Ukrainian-Canadian home and she was no more capable of promiscuity than the average housewife of similar background. A visiting comedian once tried leeringly to date her and she could hardly keep from laughing in his face. "That's the first time it's happened to me since I've been married," she told me. "I didn't know what to say."

I can remember one occasion when an outburst from Juliette startled us. But it was still one of her most regal moments.

The rift between Juliette and Bobby Gimby got worse as time went on. Gimby, already seething because he felt he wasn't getting a fair shake on the program, was reading sinister meanings into everything she said or did.

One day, prior to our regular weekly production meeting, we were looking at a kinescope of the previous Saturday's show. Sitting in a small darkened screening room, we half-watched the program. At one point, I leaned towards Julie, who was next to me, to whisper something to her—some little joke or comment that had popped into my mind. What I had failed to notice was that at that moment, Bobby Gimby's number was in progress on the screen. Julie laughed lightly at whatever it was I said, then answered in a soft voice, so as not to create any disturbance.

Bobby leaped to his feet, complaining bitterly to Bob Jarvis that "she" always talked through his number at screenings and he was getting fed up with it. Feeling guilty, I began to apologize, explaining it was my fault for talking to Julie first. But he ignored me, went on complaining to the producer.

Suddenly, from the darkness, came the queen's voice, suddenly just as impatient and angry as Gimby. In one brief sentence, not quite genteel enough to print here, she stopped Bobby in his tracks.

Gimby stalked out of the screening room and never returned to the program. (The next day, Jarvis received a call from Bobby's doctor explaining that Gimby wasn't well enough to do the show that week or perhaps for the next few weeks.)

There were, inevitably, extravagant press stories about Juliette ordering Gimby fired and so on. But this was the way it happened—no more, no less.

My own departure from the show came almost three years later, but it was neither dramatic nor angry.

About midway through my fourth year I let Bob Jarvis know that I didn't want to continue for another season. I simply wanted a change. Four years of "Silver Bells" at Christmas, "O Holy Night" for Easter and "My Buddy" on November 11 were enough. If the program was in a rut, so was I. Also, I had other projects I wanted to tackle, including the lyrics for a musical comedy. Julie didn't argue with my decision (I don't suggest she was crushed, but neither did she cheer) and we parted friends. One Toronto columnist, Nathan Cohen, felt compelled to print that I had been "dropped," even though this was denied by all concerned before he published it.

I still see her occasionally and have worked with her on occasion. When I was writing an Easter Seal show for CTV, I asked her to appear and she did, providing one of the show's highlights in a duet with Bing Crosby. I wrote a piece of material for her for a Centennial Special on CBC, which she liked and performed admirably. I even persuaded her to appear on Front Page Challenge once as a mystery guest, and she was delightful. I had the pleasure of introducing her before a huge banquet audience once, a couple of years ago, and I found myself almost tongue-tied in trying, without being maudlin, to convey what a high regard I had for her as a professional. And watching her perform that night, I took special delight in noticing the audience's excitement; they knew they were watching a star.

Jarvis stayed with the program as producer for another season, during which it went more or less along its familiar course. The following year, Mark Warren took over and tried his best to give it a new, fresh look. By using more young talent on the show, he tried to present Juliette as a kind of Ed Sullivan, sharing her spotlight with young hopefuls. It made for a different approach, but I guess it was all a bit too late. The CBC's figures showed a steady decline in ratings and eventually the Corporation decided to drop the show—after spending a year working up the courage to tell her. Juliette was hurt. She felt, naturally enough, that she should have another year—particularly with color TV coming in. But there wasn't much she could do.

Since then, she has appeared as the star of several hour-long Specials and, for the most part, received better reviews than she ever did on her regular program. She has had her own CBC radio show and she keeps as busy as she wants to with night club and banquet work. In addition, in 1968 she finally recorded her first LP (a challenge from which she had previously shied away) and sang on it better than ever.

As it happened, I didn't see the last program in her regular series until some months after it had been aired. With Mark Warren, I watched a screening of it and was truly touched by her valedictory. She handled it like a queen—a queen who was reluctantly giving up her throne but determined to depart with dignity. I found myself wishing I had written that speech for her. But then I realized nobody wrote it just that way—nobody could but Juliette.

Enter Private Enterprise

When you are seen on television across the country every week, your face and name become fairly well-known. Whether you do what you do well or badly, or whether people enjoy your show, or whether they bother to watch it—all these things have nothing to do with it; the fact is you become what is loosely termed a "celebrity." That means that you are invited to go places and do things. You are asked to talk at women's clubs (or men's service club dinners), your presence is requested at the openings of supermarkets or bowling alleys, your name is added to the endless lists of people regularly invited to cocktail parties, press conferences, literary gatherings and theatrical or night club opening nights. Since I had been a newspaper columnist for some years before I got into television, my name was already on some of those lists. But the impact of television is somehow far greater than that of the printed media. Your face on television for a few weeks makes a greater impression on people's minds than your byline in print every day for years.

Back in the days when I was doing The Barris Beat on CBC Television, I was invited to go to Moncton, New Brunswick, by the Kinsmen Club there, to be master of ceremonies at a "Car Dinner," a fund-raising affair (twenty-five dollars a plate) of which the highlight was a draw for a new automobile. The proceeds were to go towards the Kinsmen's service work; primarily aiding retarded children.

Partly because I had never been in the Maritimes, partly because their purpose made sense to me, I accepted. There was no fee or payment, but the Kinsmen paid my air fare down and back and took excellent care of me while I was there. The dinner was quite successful and it became an annual event. Since that beginning, I have been the MC at a number of similar banquets—two or three more in Moncton, and others in Sydney, N.S.; St. John's, Newfoundland; St. John, New Brunswick—usually for the Kinsmen Clubs.[1]

Quite apart from the help given to handicapped children, I've always considered such trips valuable for me. Because of them and other journeys across Canada, I have had the opportunity to visit television stations in fifteen or twenty cities and get some idea of how they operate. Besides Montreal, Ottawa, Winnipeg and Vancouver, where I've visited the CBC stations, the cities I've been to have been those with privately owned stations, thus giving me some glimpse of how private TV in Canada operates, as compared to the CBC. Their facilities are usually rather limited, which is to be expected. A station in Barrie, Ontario, say, or Sydney, N.S., neither needs nor can afford the kind of installation operated by the CBC in our eight or nine biggest Canadian cities. The programming in these private stations usually consists of news and sports news, perhaps a daily women's afternoon show, a Saturday afternoon "dance party" for teenagers, a local country music program and, of course, actuality coverage of whatever community events it can manage. The rest of the time they run movies or imported filmed shows, or network shows fed by the CBC or CTV, depending on which network they are affiliated with.

The Spartan working conditions at some of these stations are something to behold. I can remember being a guest on one show, somewhere in the Maritimes, that combined a Saturday dance party with interviews. The not-too-large studio was jammed with teenagers, dancing to recorded music. Off in a corner sat I with a couple of young people who were going to interview me. There was only one camera in the studio and the man who operated it doubled as the studio director. To get to the interview area, he had to shove his way through or around the dancing teenagers—as if he were operating a bulldozer—and hope they got out of the way in time as he advanced. Then, from behind his

---

[1] A year after the first Moncton Kinsmen Car Dinner, the same club's chapter in Agincourt, where I live, held its first similar affair. I was the MC at that and six more subsequent annual Car Dinners for the Agincourt club.

camera (and while trying to stay in focus) he had to shoot out a hand to cue the interviewers to begin. All this, of course, on the air and live.

No doubt that sort of training is good for television crews —perhaps it's the best kind—but the shaky results that sometimes occur, while acceptable at a local station, would not be tolerated by either the public or the employers on network television. I am not, by any means, belittling their efforts. Indeed, in some places I've been impressed with what they have been able to do with imagination and very little else.

At CJON, in St. John's, for example, Dan Jamieson, then co-owner of the station, used to do an excellent daily program of news, comment and interviews which had made him probably the second best-known personality in his province— right behind Joey Smallwood. And in Timmins, Ontario, CFCL owner Conrad Lavigne, an urbane and personable bilingual Canadian, used to conduct a Sunday evening program with such charm and ease that it was one of the most popular shows in the area. No doubt many other instances can be cited.

But it would be unrealistic to expect such stations to be able to produce any programs of the scope of those put on by the CBC. Even if they had the facilities and the talent, the costs would be so great the stations would be constantly losing money. Try though you may, there is no way you can make a sixty-five dollar suit look like a three hundred dollar suit. This is as true in the United States as it is in Canada. Stations in Cincinnati or Kansas City or Tulsa rely on the networks to feed them the majority of their big programming. The overwhelming majority of such programs come from either Hollywood or New York. Even if there were some sort of restriction on the amount of imported (that is, foreign) programming an American station had to carry— and I'm sure there isn't—there would be no problem posed in getting more than enough American programs to keep American viewers and American advertisers happy.

In Canada, however, things are different. From the time that the Board of Broadcast Governors came into existence in 1959, all stations have been required to carry a minimum of some fifty-five per cent of Canadian programming. There have been varying interpretations of this ruling, and it has been bent now and then, but basically it still applies. Before the second network, CTV, came into existence, the only real source of Canadian programming, apart from local shows, was the CBC. Inevitably, many private station owners were unhappy with this state of affairs. They felt, with some justification, that some of the shows fed to them were too highbrow or in some other way commercially inadequate. Yet, in order to abide by the "Canadian content" regulations, and also to fulfill their obligations as CBC affiliates, they had to take what was given them. (To some extent this situation still exists and quite possibly always will.)

Station owners and many sponsors resented the idea that a "government owned" network forced them to take programs they didn't want. Some, in fact, were simply opposed to the very idea of the government being in broadcasting, whatever the merits of the CBC programs. Quite naturally, most station owners and sponsors were champions of free enterprise and could frequently be heard—at annual association banquets and the like—urging that the government get out of television or, at the very least, allow free enterprise to compete with the CBC. From the time that Mr. Diefenbaker's Conservative government came to power, this view began to take hold inside the government and the way was gradually paved for offering the Canadian public an "alternative" to the CBC.

Thus, not too long after the creation of the Board of Broadcast Governors, the decision was made to establish "second stations" (privately owned, that is) in Canada's eight major centres. Applicants for the channels queued up eagerly, as if they were trying for licenses to print money. In fact, some foes of private TV have sometimes referred to private stations as just that: licenses to print money. However, things didn't work out quite that smoothly.

In Toronto, the area with which I'm most familiar, the winning applicant was Baton-Aldred-Rogers Broadcasting Limited. Decoded, this stood for John Bassett and John David Eaton (thus Baton), Joel Aldred, and Edward S. Rogers. The last-named was a minor figure; Bassett and Aldred were the kingpins in this marriage of convenience (earlier, both had intended to apply separately) and anybody who knows both men could confidently predict that the marriage wouldn't last. It was equally obvious that when the split came, Bassett would end up with the station—which is exactly what happened a year or so later.

Nevertheless, the partners in the venture put up an impressive station, CFTO-TV, equipped with the most up-to-date facilities for doing large-scale television programs. The biggest studio in the Agincourt (suburban Toronto) plant even had a giant electronic turntable, presumably on the strength of Joel Aldred's ability to attract such sponsors as General Motors, for whom he has done much commercial work in the United States. Such turntables are sometimes used in automobile commercials.

Some good people were recruited for the new station, including Murray Chercover, a CBC producer, and Rai Purdy, a veteran broadcaster. But almost from the beginning the in-fighting began and over the following months there were shake-ups, the rolling of heads, re-organizations, budget slashing, wars and rumors of wars. First Purdy was gone, then Aldred. After a lot of smoke had cleared away, John Bassett stood firmly in command.

My own experience with CFTO began, in a way, before its birth. Long before the BBG had decided which of the several Toronto applicants would get the second license in the city, I approached Mr. Bassett about doing the late-night show I had heard the new station was planning. By this time I was writing my column for the *Telegram*, which is also owned by Mr. Bassett.

A number of people were auditioned for the show, myself included. The station finally chose Rick Campbell to do it. However, I was asked to do another program—fifteen minutes twice a week on the entertainment scene in Toronto. Like my column in the *Telegram*, this was called "The Barris Beat."

The station was to go on the air January 1, 1961, with a huge telethon to raise money for crippled children. Every effort was made to recruit entertainers and celebrities for it.[1]

---

[1] One of the CFTO producers was assigned to approach Wayne and Shuster to appear on the telethon. He had the misfortune to telephone Wayne, the more volatile partner. Wayne considered the request an imposition, largely because the comedy team had been identified with the CBC for so many years. Wayne blasted the producer, who tried to defend himself by pointing out that he was only carrying out orders. "You sonofabitch," snapped Johnny, "that's what Eichmann said."

It's tough enough to get a new station on the air more or less smoothly, but to do it with a twelve- or fifteen-hour telethon is like trying to launch D-Day while an Olympiad is being held in the same place. Still, it came off reasonably well.

Following the giant telethon, CFTO was to begin its regular schedule of programming, which included a kiddies' show, a noontime variety show, a modest public affairs show, the late night program, plus news and sports. With that sort of load, my tacky little fifteen-minute program must have seemed rather insignificant to those at the new station hustling about trying to get everything ready for D-Day.

Still, I was a little unnerved when I went in for a rehearsal, a few days before the station opening. The studio in which I was to work was hardly bigger than the third bedroom of a suburban house—perhaps fifteen feet long and eleven feet wide. A handsomely painted Toronto skyline scene was my "set." In front of this was a stool with a tiny stand, just about large enough to hold a portable typewriter. Facing the spot where I was to sit was one television camera pedestal—and perched atop the pedestal was a cardboard box marked "camera." The camera itself, I was assured, would be there by opening day. It reminded me of those pictures you used to see early in the Second World War of army recruits carrying broom sticks in lieu of rifles.

The camera was there on the day of my first show, but my guest wasn't. In the fifteen-minute program I was to give news of entertainment activity in town and then chat with a guest, some visiting performer or local entertainer each time. I don't recall who was scheduled to be the guest on that first program, but he got caught up in rush-hour traffic (the station is located some seventeen miles from downtown Toronto) and simply didn't get there. Joel Aldred was hastily recruited to substitute, and he turned out to be a good guest. The scheduled guest, incidentally, turned up just as we were finishing the program.

Working in that tiny studio over the following months was a traumatic experience. To begin with, doing any TV show (except for a straight newscast) with one camera is ridiculous. But a second camera wouldn't fit into that studio, anyway. Any time I wanted to show a picture of somebody in the entertainment news, I had to hold it up, steadily, if possible, while the camera moved in for a close shot of it, then backed up again to include me in the shot. When a guest arrived he had to crowd in on a second stool next to me and the cameraman was practically up the back wall in an attempt to have a wide enough shot to take in both of us.

But there was more fun. The show went on the air at six-fifteen. We used to do a "rehearsal" at about four-thirty. I say "about" because the starting time for my rehearsal depended on how quickly the crew could remove the set of an earlier show done in the same studio. That spacious phone booth sure earned its keep. Then I realized the whole business of rehearsing my show was academic. You see, the cameraman who was there for the rehearsal went off duty at five or five-thirty and a different cameraman—who had not been present for the rehearsal—came on duty in time to shoot my show on the air—live. It was a little bit like having a stand-in for the surgeon who's going to operate on your heart.

But try though I did to get the station to reshuffle its work schedule in order to avoid this idiocy, I had no success. Twice a week, week after week, I went on the air with a cameraman who had not been present for the rehearsal; while, so far as I knew, the one who had was at home chuckling over the disastrous results of his absence. And so, in that incredible little studio I interviewed such guests as Dizzy Gillespie, Gratien Gelinas, Hollywood actor Don Murray, Bruno Gerussi, Walter Susskind and Broadway star Gretchen Wyler. I could often imagine one or another of them returning home and saying, "You wouldn't believe the studio I was in in Toronto. . . ." After some twenty-six weeks. my program was changed to a thirty-minute show once a week and we were moved into one of the larger studios with two cameras. Things went somewhat more smoothly then and I felt better about doing the program.

In August, however, Murray Chercover, then program director of the station, told me they wanted to take my show off in the fall for the football season and that it would resume "around the end of the year." I felt this was unsatisfactory, in that no program can build and maintain an audience unless it is seen regularly and in the same time slot. So we agreed to drop the whole thing at the conclusion of the cycle. I did my program for thirty-nine weeks and that was the end of that.

During that first year or two of existence, CFTO was having its problems—mostly financial. Running a private station in a large metropolitan area was not, after all, a "license to print money." The fact was that the splendid CFTO plant was, for those early years, rather more splendid than was needed. Sponsors didn't grow on trees for a private station any more than they did for the CBC. Having elaborate studios was one thing; being able to afford elaborate shows in those studios was another. Little by little, many of the station's ambitious plans were scrubbed. A daytime soap opera, slaved over for months in the preparation, never went on the air. The noontime variety show was dropped. A couple of panel-game shows were tried out but soon killed. "Better Late," the late-night show with Rick Campbell, was eventually dropped. Another late-night show, done in association with CTV and involving segments from other cities, failed to make it.

Of course, things got better eventually. Coverage of sports events was successful, as were a series of inexpensively produced daytime quiz shows, usually coproduced with such outside packagers as Roy Ward Dickson. More recently, public affairs and variety shows of merit have improved the station's Canadian content level.

Since those early days, my experience with CFTO has been limited. On one occasion, I was asked to write the Easter Seal Show, a benefit for all those involved in it. I couldn't resist the request when I learned that the headliner was to be Bing Crosby. He had been an idol of mine when I was a youngster and the opportunity to work with him could not be passed up. The experience was a rewarding one. Crosby was gentlemanly, considerate, patient, co-operative—everything you half expect a big star not to be.

Another time, I was asked to work with producer Jerry Rochon on a CFTO Special about the National Youth Orchestra. The idea for the show was a good one. We would select one member of the orchestra and cover its activities through her eyes. In the interest of Canadian solidarity, it was decided to seek a French-Canadian girl, so Jerry and I spent several days in Montreal and Quebec City interviewing female members of the orchestra who might fit the requirements. We found a perfectly delightful girl in Montreal and Jerry and I were eagerly looking forward to doing the show.

But complications developed. Because quite a few members of the Youth Orchestra were also members of the musicians' union, the union felt the musicians must be paid for the TV program. This the station was prepared to do, but officials of the Youth Orchestra felt that the nonprofessional members of the orchestra must not be paid. There seemed no way to resolve the conflict, so the whole program had to be shelved.

It may seem surprising that a private station like CFTO would be willing, or even able, to pay the members of a large symphony orchestra for a television special. But CFTO and, to a lesser extent, other private stations, will go on such spending sprees from time to time, mostly, I've always suspected, to keep the Board of Broadcast Governors (or its successor, the Canadian Radio-Television Commission) appeased.

CFTO produces an annual Christmas program featuring the Toronto Symphony. It has, on one occasion, done a full-scale Shakespearean drama (*Henry V*) in co-operation with the Stratford Festival. It also put on a ninety-minute original drama, *A Rumble of Silence,* starring Kate Reid.

But such specials are put on by private stations rather infrequently. They are status symbols on which the stations clearly lose money. Some of them have been excellent and and I have the greatest admiration for those stations which try—however infrequently—to put on some Canadian programs of genuine merit. It is still a fact, however, that for the most part privately owned stations in Canada cannot afford to do very much Canadian programming on a large scale. The CBC can do it (and whether or not they do it well is another argument) because, of course, the CBC gets government money.

Before there was private television of any significant size, people in television used to complain that the trouble was you "couldn't go across the street." That is, in the United States or England, if you couldn't get the money or the program conditions you wanted at one network you could try another. There was and is competition; free enterprise stimulates incentive; a good program idea or a talented performer can make the networks bid against each other. And so on. The theory was that when second stations and a second network opened in Canada, programs would improve and opportunities for creative Canadians would increase. The theory was, on the whole, nonsense. You still can't go across the street. There is nothing much there except buildings, facilities, studios—but no budgets.

This not because private television is "cheap." It is simply because private television means no public money, no income but that brought in through the sale of programs to sponsors, and therefore the constant restriction of putting on only such programs as can be sold. Except for those "Specials" which are produced when private television figures it's time to impress the authorities—not so much the public—with its good intentions and its creative ability.

And so we are back, like it or not, to the one-sided street. Private enterprise, for reasons to be gone into at more length later in this book, has not come riding in on its white charger to save Princess Television from the clutches of the bureaucrats. As the old saying has it, when you're a gambler you play, even though you know the only game in town is fixed. Sixteen years after the birth of television in Canada, the CBC still runs the only game in town. So we play, knowing it's fixed, but hoping that somehow we might manage to switch the dice.

What Do You Do on Front Page Challenge?

In the summer of 1964 I took my family to Europe for a two-month holiday. It was a memorable summer, despite the fact that it was slightly marred by ill-health. I had a kidney stone that refused to go away. As soon as we returned, I made arrangements to go into hospital for an operation to remove the stone. The day I was to go into Scarborough General Hospital, I received a telephone call from Don Brown, a producer at the CBC, asking me if I could drop in to see him that afternoon. That was impossible, but we managed—in a series of telephone talks before, almost during and after my operation—to get together on a contract for me to become the writer of Front Page Challenge that fall.

The program had by then been on the air for some six years and continued to be one of the most successful on the CBC. I had occasionally appeared on it as a guest panelist, but apart from that had had no regular connection with it since the first summer it was on the air, when I worked as a regular panelist and, more briefly, as its moderator. Brown was new to the program and, as is usually the case, wanted to make some minor changes. He felt my newspaper background would be valuable to the show.

As a result of his initial call, I entered an arrangement which made me a regular visitor to the Pierce-Arrow Showroom again for the next four years. For despite the existence of the vastly superior Studio Seven, Front Page Challenge was necessarily one of the shows still done regularly at the awful barn on Yonge Street. But writing the show was a stimulating experience and offered again the opportunity to meet all sorts of fascinating people—from world-famous political figures to home-grown eccentrics.

During that time, one of the questions I was asked most often, by people I met outside the television business, was: "What is Gordon Sinclair really like?" But the question I was asked even more often was: "What do you do on Front Page Challenge?" Behind it was a certain understandable skepticism. One sees the credits whiz by at the end of a program and notices that a credit reads "Written by Alex Barris." This sometimes jars the viewer. Does this mean the show is "fixed?" How can those electric confrontations between Sinclair and the lady evangelist or the petty politician be "written"?

Though I've answered it many times, I'll try once more. In a sense, the term "writer" is misleading in television. In the case of a drama or a situation comedy show or even a documentary, one can easily comprehend the writer's function. In other areas it isn't so clear. On a musical variety show, for example, "writing" consists of more than putting down on paper the relatively few words the host says to the guest, or the introduction to this song or that. It involves much more: helping to plan the show, often suggesting not only the songs to be sung and the guests to sing them, but the way the guests and songs are to be presented visually. The writer must be concerned with the look of a set, though not its execution; with the style or mood of a musical arrangement; with the pacing of a show—what sort of number should follow this one, should there be a sketch here or a dance number?

True, all these things are also the concern of the producer and ultimately it is he who makes the decisions. The writer is, therefore, a kind of right arm to the producer, an assistant or associate, a sounding board, an idea man, a person who (if he is earning his salt) will argue with the producer whenever he disagrees with anything—from what a singer should wear to how an actor should move. I have heard producers claim that they are, in essence, writers. I have yet to hear one acknowledge that the writer is, in essence, an associate to the producer. Yet, this is really what the writer's function is—to assist the producer in planning, thinking out and realizing the show.

When it comes to a program like Front Page Challenge, the same general description applies. True, the amount of "writing" is minimal. The writer of the program simply turns in a skeletal script, which the moderator (Fred Davis, in this case) more or less follows. But that is the least of the writer's concerns. He is present at meetings in which shows are planned. He must bring in suggestions for guests or stories—as, of course, will the producer, the researcher and others.[1] The producer will look to the writer for some opinion on the merits of a potential story or challenger: we need a lighter story here, to balance an otherwise serious show; would it be better to try to get this political figure or that one to represent a certain story? what sort of guest panelist will best help to draw out a given challenger?

Once the show's content is decided on, the writer has the responsibility of supervising the editing of film to be used in "recreating" the story, and the writing of the announcer's commentary which is spoken while the film is shown. When challengers arrive in the studio, the writer and researchers will go over this "script" with them, to make sure they understand the nature of the show and that the information in the script that accompanies the film is essentially accurate. And, finally, the writer also prepares a list of questions on each story, to be given to the panel (*after* the guessing game is over) in case they need ammunition with which to confront the challengers during the interview that follows.

It is, I think, enough of a job, one that is hardly adequately explained by the term "written by" but an important one nevertheless. One day, perhaps someone will come up with a more accurate word to describe the function of a writer of such television shows, but for the time being it will have to do. During my years with Front Page Challenge, one of the happy by-products was the chance to meet and often share a dinner with a seemingly endless parade of engaging people.

There were sports celebrities like Nancy Greene, Bobby Hull, Gordie Howe, George Knudsen and Bernie Faloney. There were many Canadian political figures, from Louis St. Laurent and Lester Pearson to Dalton Camp and René

---

[1] On this as on other panel shows, suggestions from viewers tend to dry up as the show goes on year after year. People send in ideas we have already used; some have a good story idea but the wrong challenger, or vice versa. Most of the useable suggestions originate in the production meetings.

Levesque. (Only John Diefenbaker consistently refused to appear on the program, apparently because it was sponsored.) There were such controversial figures as Mark Lane, the Duke of Bedford, Dr. Benjamin Spock, Christine Jorgenson, Ralph Nader and Dr. Timothy Leary. And there were more glamorous celebrities like Bennett Cerf, Victor Borge, Pearl Mesta, Arthur Hailey, Risë Stevens, Groucho Marx, Artie Shaw and Ethel Merman.

As was the case with One Of A Kind, not every guest proved to be lovable. One of the more colorful ones was "Ma" Murray, that gritty old woman from British Columbia who published her own newspaper. Colorful she was, but at dinner I found her narrow-minded.

Ethel Merman, the trumpet-voiced veteran of Broadway and Hollywood, was troublesome in another way. She was invited to appear on the show in May, 1967, when we were doing two programs from Expo 67. Her manager agreed to the offer, but said Miss Merman would require a hotel suite for a three-day period. Hotel suites in Montreal were not easy to come by a month after the opening of Expo, but we managed. When the lady arrived, she was given a cheque to cover her hotel suite for three days, in addition to her fee. But she had no intention of staying in Montreal that long. Still, she took both cheques and, incidentally, didn't even pay her hotel bill. The CBC, which is too often intimidated by such brassy behavior from imported stars, paid the bill.

Of the hundreds of challengers who appeared on the program during my four years with it, only one refused at almost the last moment to go on. That was Pietro Annigoni, the Italian portrait painter who gained some fame through his portrait of Princess Margaret. There was some silly misunderstanding involving the time he would be required at the studio. When he learned he would have to spend an hour longer than he'd expected, he stalked out in a huff. He was located at the nearby home of a friend, but flatly refused to return to the studio. Fortunately, we had planned three stories for that show instead of two, so we simply stretched the two interviews out to fill the half-hour and nobody really missed Signor Annigoni. (I was all for suing the man for breach of contract, but the CBC never does anything so crude.)

I found that although such noted funnymen as Victor Borge and Groucho Marx were welcome guests for the audience, they were not as far as the panelists were concerned. Even people like Gordon Sinclair and Pierre Berton feel insecure around comics and are afraid to speak up because they expect to be used as "straight-men." Also relatively unwelcome were sports figures. With rare exceptions, we found our panelists were not much interested in sports and their boredom tended to show. This could sometimes be avoided by bringing in sports-oriented guest panelists (like Bill Stephenson or Trent Frayne) but the disadvantage here was that their appearance was a dead giveaway to the regular panelists, who were then alerted to expect a sports story. On the whole, I think the best guest panelists the program has used are Lister Sinclair and Lorraine Thomson. They have made many guest appearances and never failed to add substantially to the success of the programs they have graced.

One of the more frustrating aspects of working on the program was the occasional clash with the CBC's public affairs department. Let me explain that Front Page Challenge is produced by the light entertainment department. But much of its strength derives from the appearance of challengers involved in past or present stories of vital concern to the public. The public affairs department is something of a little empire within the CBC and its leaders had actually persuaded the CBC that no "light entertainment" program should be permitted to use public figures without first getting the approval of the public affairs department. This meant we had to go, hat in hand, to ask if it would be permissible for us to use a Walter Gordon or a Daniel Johnson. The way it sometimes worked out, if some public affairs program was planning to use such a person in, say, two or three weeks, our request was turned down. Of course, any public affairs producer might occasionally make use of a Sammy Davis or some other entertainer appearing in Toronto. At such times, no one ever had to check with light entertainment for "permission" to employ such a guest. What they did was their business. What *we* did was also their business. But not the other way around.

Such inconveniences aside, Front Page Challenge has

always been an interesting show to be involved in. And I always looked forward to the pre-show dinner with the guests. At one such dinner, one of our guests was Sir Alec Douglas-Home, once the prime minister of Britain. He was an urbane man and in good spirits. At dinner, he kept the rest of us fascinated with his stories. Sir Alec had ordered fish and when it was brought he was in mid-anecdote, so he absently picked up a knife and fork and began to separate the fish as he talked. The waiter who had served him suddenly reached over and grabbed the knife out of Sir Alec's hand. "That's not for fish," he scolded, "this one is for fish." And he handed another knife to the former prime minister of Britain. The rest of us were dumbfounded, but Sir Alec was too much of a gentleman to argue with the tactless waiter. He merely took the proffered knife, said "Thank you," and went right on with his story.

For some time these dinners were held at the Ports of Call, a florid restaurant complex located close to the Pierce-Arrow Showroom. What made us move (to the Park Plaza) was the forgetfulness of Gordon Sinclair and, to a lesser extent, of Pierre Berton. Our panelists knew that the Ports of Call was off limits to them because that was where we took the guests to dine. Yet, on at least one occasion, Berton "forgot" and went there for a drink or a bite, at roughly the same time when we were in one of the dining rooms with that evening's challengers. He did not see them, but it was too close for comfort.

As for Gordon, he "forgot" more than once. I remember one evening in particular when he walked in and sauntered over to a corner table. We and our guests were midway through dinner across the room. Roger McKean, who is employed by the program to look after guests during their stay in Toronto, was obliged to go over to Sinclair's table and remind him that he really wasn't supposed to be there. Gordon got up and walked out, looking about as innocent as a hockey player on his way to the penalty box. I know this business sounds sneaky, but I could never be angry with Sinclair. It's part of his make-up, this determination to look good on the show, to be able to come up with the answers. In fact, Sinclair's value to the program has always been so great that nobody would really care if he never guessed the identity of a challenger. It's in the salty interviews that follow where Sinclair shines.

I've known Gordon for almost two decades and I've grown to like him. He is, it's true, a most exasperating newsman—terribly opinionated, sometimes shockingly inaccurate, often passionately devoted to the nuttiest of causes, illogically opposed to many reasonable ones.[1] But there is not a mean bone in his body. I have never known him to willingly do harm to anyone but the most flagrant phonies or crooks. Despite his toughness with some challengers, Gordon is a pussycat. Most important of all, Gordon Sinclair is colorful. He is a Canadian original. People may hate him, but they cannot resist him. Even those who hate him will tune him in, hoping to see him get his comeuppance.

In my opinion, Gordon is the single most valuable element in the success of Front Page Challenge. In its dozen years on the air, he has missed only a few shows (consecutively, by the way) and that was because of an illness. He loves doing the program and I believe the show will remain on the air as long as Sinclair's health holds up. Ironically, he feels insecure. Each year, when contract renewal time is at hand, he worries if his contract is late. He takes seriously periodic rumors that he is going to be replaced on the show. Nobody in his right mind—and there are still some of those at the CBC—would dream of dumping Sinclair.

Gordon is obsessed with the importance of money, as anyone knows who has heard, seen or read him. He is, of course, well off, to put it mildly. If he never earned another nickel, he could live out his days in comfort. His children are provided for and, in any case, are all earning their own incomes. Yet he frets over money. He grumbles about taxation, but takes a curious pride in never having formed a personal corporation (as so many of his colleagues in TV have done) in order to have a better tax position. He stews over the stock market, he blasts governments for spending too much of "his" money, he snarls over the failure of governments to

---

[1] For years, Sinclair has publicly picked on the Hospital For Sick Children and opposed that hospital's periodic drives for funds. The reason, though illogical, was personal and sadly human: many years ago, his young daughter was taken there when she was struck down by a car; she never recovered and Gordon has never forgiven the hospital.

tax churches, he gripes about free-loaders and wastrels who expect handouts.

A few years ago, when he was sixty-five, we had a little party for Gordon. It was a pleasant gathering and we had fun ribbing him while we presented him with gifts and words of affection. The highlight of the evening came when Sinclair responded to the toasts and roasts. Suddenly, he was in a serious, reflective mood. He touched on the subject of money and the fact that he has always been kidded for his inordinate interest in it. What followed then was a vivid description of his childhood, which was anything but comfortable. It was then that he had grasped the importance of money and this conviction was to shape his thinking for the rest of his life.

Gordon is not, of course, alone in that view. The difference between him and so many of us is that he freely admits it. More than that, because he is colorful and outspoken and because he has access to the public through broadcasting, his views are widely known and oft repeated. So, for that matter, are other Sinclair views. He is an atheist and delights in needling those with conventional religious beliefs. He is unabashedly pro-Canadian and never feels a trace of embarrassment about proclaiming it. He is violently opposed to fluoridation of drinking water ("rat poison," he calls it) and most other experiments in public health. He loves to wear impossibly loud clothing and once told me I looked like a mortician because my jacket and trousers matched. He is, to many people, a character, an eccentric, a braggart, a loudmouth, a disgrace. The one thing he is not and never will be is dull.

Thus far, I haven't said much about the others on the show. Next to Gordon, I think the key person is Fred Davis. Television critics can dismiss him all they want to as being bland or mechanical. Those connected with the show have a high regard for his professionalism. I know of nobody in this country—and possibly outside it—who can pilot a panel show as smoothly as Fred can. Countless times, he has been in the awkward spot of winding up a heated, sometimes ugly discussion. Unfailingly, he manages to smooth things over and move on to the next item without betraying any suggestion of discomfort. If there is any insincerity in Davis it is only in the extent to which he suppresses on camera the more informal side of his nature. He is so proper, so correct, so capable, so well-mannered that even the moments when he must think quickly to smooth over a blemish in the show seem simple. He can be much hipper, much glibber, much wittier and much more fun than TV audiences are ever given reason to suspect. Davis, a compulsive backer of worthy causes, manages to appeal to just about everybody. He is not only liked but, as Willy Loman used to say, well liked. Anyone who can have admirers in both the I.O.D.E. and C.O.R.E. can't be all b.a.d. The fact is he's a very nice man, serious but not humorless about his work, genuinely interested in the various causes he openly supports, coldly logical about his career but warmly concerned about the problems of other people.

In her way, Betty Kennedy is very similar to Fred. She, too, is a polished professional. Her widely heard daily broadcasts on CFRB reflect the range of her interests. Although she does not advertise it, Betty does a good deal of speaking before clubs and societies. She accepts no fee, but requires that each such organization make a donation to the Save the Children Fund.

The only person regularly on Front Page Challenge who remains an enigma to me is Pierre Berton. While I recognize his ability as a commentator and writer, I have always felt a lack of warmth in him, an absence of compassion. He is concerned with issues but not the people involved in them, with Man but not men.[1] I suppose he fits the role of the "bad guy" on the show. Sure, Sinclair does a lot of ranting and raving, but that isn't the same. It's Berton who coldly goes after the challenger. The only trouble is that he sometimes seems just as cold and aloof when the person being interviewed is not a fraud, a politician, or a bigot. Perhaps I'm being unfair. Berton and I have never been good friends, but neither have we ever been enemies. I have spent neither more nor less time with him than with the others on the show. I have

---

[1]Edmund Wilson, the esteemed American author and critic, was once in Toronto for a lecture and was persuaded to appear with Berton on his own Pierre Berton Show which was being video-taped that day. On his way to the airport after the program, Wilson was asked what he thought of Berton. The man of letters smiled a bit sadly and said, "I'm afraid your Mr. Berton wasn't terribly interested in me."

rarely mixed with them socially, for no particular reason other than that they have their friends and I have mine. My impressions of all of them are, for the most part, based on the regular contact I have had with them in connection with Front Page Challenge.

Two other veterans with the program are Lucio Agostini, its musical director, and Benard Cowan, its chief announcer. Cowan, a highly successful commercial announcer who is also active in radio and television production outside the CBC, is the man whose mellow voice accompanies the film "recreating" each story on the show. He has been associated with Front Page Challenge since it began in 1957 and has always served it well. Agostini, one of the ablest musicians in Canada, has also been with Challenge since its birth. His role is to compose and orchestrate the background music that accompanies the aforementioned film. In the past dozen years, he has had to write about one thousand bits of original music, each running about one minute long. Only once can I remember Lucio making an error and it turned out to be funny, if also unintentionally "sick." We were doing a story on the Bay of Pigs invasion and, for some reason, the script was late getting to Lucio. (He needed it to gauge the mood and length of the music required to accompany the film.) In his haste, he noticed that the story was datelined Havana but obviously did not read further. The result was that when we ran the film with music and commentary, the ugly scenes of bombs bursting and bodies falling were accompanied by a gay, carefree rhumba. Fortunately, this was in the rehearsal and the embarrassed Mr. Agostini was able to change the music in time for the show.

Also unseen by the home audience but vital to the program is the man who "warms up" the studio audience. For the past few years, this has been done by Paul Kligman, an experienced actor and comic. Before Paul came to the show, the warmup was done by Larry Mann, who now lives and works in Hollywood. Both men are well qualified for this work, but I remember with particular fondness one night when Larry Mann shone. Like many such programs, Front Page Challenge shows are done two in one evening. One show goes on the air "live" and the other is taped for telecast the following week. (Thus, studio facilities and personnel are tied up only once every two weeks.) Normally, there is about a 15-minute break between programs and the warmup man again must keep the studio audience amused during this lull in activity, as he has done when they first arrived.

On this night, Victor Borge was a challenger and the time of the taped show had to be moved up to seven-thirty, instead of the usual taping time of eight-forty-five, so that Borge could get to O'Keefe Centre in time for his nightly show there. This meant a gap of an hour and a half between the end of the taped show and the start of the live one. Mann was charged with keeping that studio audience happy for all that time. He was magnificent. He told stories, answered questions, gave away gag gifts, clowned, stalled, ad libbed, interviewed spectators and somewhow managed to use up all that time. It was a superior, spontaneous one man show, and only a couple of hundred studio spectators saw it.

The other key person on Front Page Challenge is, naturally, the producer. During my years with the program Don Brown has performed that function. I have found him on the whole an easy man to work with. This is not to say we always agreed. Many of our production meetings were marked by explosive arguments. But he has the virtue of understanding that this is partly what I'm paid for. He often ribbed me about interrrupting him or taking over the meeting or arguing too passionately; but he always recognized that this was part of my job and that merely agreeing with him to keep peace would have been a disservice to the program.

After four years with Front Page Challenge, my future with the program became uncertain. This was because I was to be involved in a new program of my own, called Barris & Company, the following fall. Don Brown was reluctant to lose my services and wanted me to continue with his show as well as doing mine, but it became evident that I would not be able to devote my full energies to the new undertaking and also give full value to Don's program.

A compromise was finally worked out. I would begin the 1968/69 season with Front Page Challenge, working with Jack Hutchinson, who was being brought in as a second writer and researcher. I would guide Jack in learning the routine of the program and then gradually withdraw from it.

But since my contact for the new program was limited to thirteen weeks with options—standard procedure in television—we reached an understanding that if the new show did not continue beyond the first thirteen weeks, I would return to Front Page Challenge.

As the young man in the hair cream commercial says, I came back.

Anatomy of a Failure

There is a standard Hollywood writers' story that is known as "It's Always Cesar Romero." It goes like this. Producer calls in writer and tells him of big picture he's planning to make starring Gregory Peck. He wants writer to do script. Writer goes home to slave over hot typewriter, delivers sizzling script tailor-made for Peck. Producer loves it but tells writer Peck is unavailable. Script must be rewritten to suit Tony Curtis. Another rewrite, another disappointment. Curtis can't do it. Write it again, this time for Anthony Perkins. Back to the typewriter, but this time Perkins is out and Van Johnson is in. One more time. Great script, only now the producer wants a further rewrite—Johnson is out, but the producer is sure the film is just right for Cesar Romero.

On his way back to the typewriter, the dizzy writer recalls that he has been through all this before and he faces the sad truth: it's always Cesar Romero. The names change, but the story has happened a thousand times, and not always in Hollywood. I remembered it when I began to reflect on the birth, short life and inevitable death of a CBC series in which I was involved a few years ago. It was called "A World of Music."

We started out, hopelessly optimistic, with talk of Gregory Pecks and ended up, heads bloody and bowed, with a Cesar Romero. To some extent or other, I know that many ambitious show-business projects turn out somewhat smaller, shallower and sadder than they appeared to be in the dream stage. But the case of A World of Music stands alone, in my own experience at least, as a towering medley of mistakes from start to finish, a snowball of errors that grew and gathered momentum as it hurtled downhill until it crashed against an immovable rock of reality. A chronicle of its brief, unhappy life deserves inclusion here not only because it was part of my experience in the unreal world of television, but also because it might shed some light on how a new television series is sometimes put together—even a bad one.

In the spring of 1966, Bob Jarvis called me into his office and asked me what I thought of the idea of Malka and Joso fronting a new series featuring international folk music. I said it sounded fine. (I have tried since to examine honestly my motives. It's true I had, only a week or two before, decided to give up my column for the *Telegram* and devote my full time as a freelance writer to television. But that wasn't all. I really did believe there was a growing market for international music; I really did feel that the size of the "New Canadian" population warranted some television entertainment not only aimed at them but reflecting their presence in Canada and the wealth of their cultural contribution to Canada's future.)

The reason for Jarvis's question, it developed, was that the CBC had decided to drop the Juliette Show at the end of that season and was looking around for a replacement to start in the fall. Despite Juliette's understandable bitterness, she was not dropped to "make way" for A World of Music. Whatever the merits of the decision to drop her show, that decision was made. A World of Music was then created to fill a void.

The CBC's light entertainment department planned to do a series of twelve summer shows—each one different, each one intended as a kind of pilot which, if it worked, might be chosen as the replacement series for the Juliette spot. But from the outset, Jarvis felt that the Malka and Joso idea was the most promising, if only because it offered a marked contrast to the conventional popular music usually heard on television variety shows.

The dozen pilot shows were done (including ours) but even before they got on the air it was decided that A World of Music, with Malka and Joso, would be replacing Juliette. Jarvis no doubt helped steer the choice in that direction, but the decision itself was made at a higher level and with the eventual, if dubious, approval of the sponsors who bought it. Not long after my initial talk with Jarvis, there was a sudden rush to plan the Malka and Joso pilot and to prepare a presentation brochure, outlining the concept of the show. Handsome color pictures were obtained and I had to write the blurbs for this brochure, which was to help "sell" the series. Feeling as we did, Jarvis and I tackled the job with enthusiasm.

Oh, what glorious dreams we had. Among the internationally renowned guests we "planned" to have were Sergio Franchi, Nana Mouskouri, Caterina Valente, Theodore Bikel, Miriam Makeba and Carlos Montoya. Research was done and arguments presented about the potential size of the audience for such a show—one-third of Canada's people, after all, are of neither French nor British origin, but Germans, Italians, Ukrainians, Hungarians, Greeks, et cetera.

The appeal of Malka and Joso needed little selling, it seemed. In two years together they had gained a good reputation in coffee houses (mostly in Toronto and Montreal) and concert tours with their repertory of songs in seven or eight languages. They had already recorded a couple of LPs and were slated to do more. Malka Himel, born in Israel, was dark and strikingly beautiful, spoke with a charming continental accent, stood proud and regal. Joso Spraljia, from Jugosolavia, was a handsome, bearded troubadour, musically gifted but shy—the virile, silent type.[1] Bob Jarvis was to produce and direct the pilot, I was signed to write it, with an option to be the regular writer if the show went on the air, and Rudy Toth, a fine and experienced musician, was chosen as musical director.

The pilot show, all too hastily done so that it might be available for selling purposes, was not a raging success. Still, everyone involved had faith in the idea of the show—and the decision to go on with it had already been made, anyway. At this distance in time, it's much easier to see the mistakes we all made. For example, it was never intended that Jarvis would produce the series because he was committed to other projects, notably a series of one-hour specials called "O'Keefe Centre Presents." So Mark Warren, who had produced the

---

[1] What we took for his shyness, in our early meetings with him, turned out to be an almost total inability to speak in English, beyond a few words.

last two years of the Juliette Show, was assigned to A World of Music.

An assignment under these circumstances is difficult. Warren had no hand in the pilot, nothing to say about whether he thought Malka and Joso could or should front a show, no part in selecting either his writer or his musical director. In fact, he hardly knew any of us. Having worked with Juliette, he had come to know and respect Lucio Agostini, her musical director for those last two years. It is no reflection on Rudy Toth's ability (or Mark's appraisal of it) that Mark would naturally have preferred to continue working with Lucio. The same might well have applied to his feelings about the choice of writer, although we got along well and Mark never, by word or action, suggested any displeasure about working with me.[1] Mark's own background has a bearing on the matter, too. He is a young man, from the United States, bright, modern in his outlook, interested in today's music. It would be extraordinary to expect him to have any special feeling for folk music from Israel, Italy or Russia.

A far more serious mistake was the choice of the time slot for the show—although I cannot claim to have realized this at the time. Nobody involved in the show did, at first. The spot following the Saturday night hockey telecasts is a tricky one. The program in that time slot "inherits" the largest television audience in Canada. Holding it is something else. We were soon to find out that the three or four million hockey fans who were our inherited audience had no interest in Malka and Joso, their music or their guests. The mail, though not great in volume, was sometimes ugly—they didn't want "foreigners," they disliked "that Jewess," they had no interest in folk songs done in half a dozen languages they didn't understand.

And, of course, our show never lived up to those glowing promises we made to the sponsors and their agencies. We soon realized—and should have known all along—that we simply could not afford most of the name guests we dreamed of using. Stars like Sergio Franchi or Caterina Valente can

---

[1] Ken Gunton, once a CBC studio director and more recently a director of TV commercials, was taken on as a second writer. It was his first writing assignment, but we found we worked well together.

get $5,000 or $7,500 to appear on an Ed Sullivan or Dean Martin Show. Why would they bother to come to Canada for $1,000 or even $1,500? We tried, but we had fallen right into the Cesar Romero trap. If not Sergio Franchi, how about Enzo Stuarti? No? Then, maybe someone not as "big." We had some good guests, like Astrud Gilberto, Josh White, Buffy St. Marie, the Beers Family—not exactly traffic-stopping "names" but talented and available. Cesar Romeros.

But the biggest mistake, I guess, was trying to fit this round musical peg into the square-hole audience accustomed to moving lazily from hockey action to hokey music. In truth, a European artist of Nana Mouskouri's stature would probably have been no more impressive to that audience than some of the unknown European-born performers we found in Canada.

Mark and I spent considerable time during the summer months auditioning potential guest acts. In Toronto we watched and listened to every imaginable type of entertainer —from German dancers in lederhosen to Greek bouzouki players; from gypsy violinists to Caribbean limbo dancers; from Alpine polka groups to Spanish flamenco guitarists. We went to Montreal to audition French singers and Mexican mariachis and Haitian singers and Italian accordionists and Japanese koto players. We auditioned vocal groups and dancers and instrumentalists in Vancouver. We listened to Ukrainian comedians and German lieder singers and Israeli crooners in Winnipeg. We heard Portuguese fado and saw Scottish sword dancing. We auditioned platoons of Poles, regiments of Roumanians, brigades of Balkans, armies of Africans, hordes of Hungarians, waves of West Indians. We attended a mammoth festival of "ethnic" entertainers and took copious notes as to the merits of each.

Very little of this world of talent ever got in front of a camera on A World of Music. The mistake had been made of assuming that the available audience would be interested in that kind of show. Once we realized they might not be, mistake was piled on mistake. The main one was to start compromising.

Compromise is the pitfall of the arts, the trap that awaits any showman confronted with the potential apathy of his audience. Well, the theory goes, if they don't like this we'll give them that. If we can't grab the whole audience with one act, we'll do it with another. It masquerades under the name of variety, but it is a sign of panic—a Cesar Romero. And tied to it is another error. Wait a minute, now, let's not go overboard. Suppose they don't dig Ukrainian songs; let's be smart and toss in an Irish step dance. Maybe the flamenco dance is too esoteric; let's follow it with an English ballad. How do we know they'll appreciate an Israeli work song; let's have her do it in English, or at least French, and play it safe. This, too, masquerades as variety, but it is really a retreat, a copping out.

Like all compromises (in the arts, anyway) it leads to failure. The moment you start worrying about offending someone, you end up pleasing no one. The minute you try being all shows to all audiences, you wind up with no viewers. The second you try sugar-coating the pill you were so sure was going to sell, you remind the buyer it was a pill he didn't need in the first place. We did our share of sugar-coating. We hired dancers to fill up our set. We cajoled Malka and Joso into singing more "familiar" songs. We used guest acts that had no business on that show—in terms of its original purpose—other than to offset possible audience resistance to the show itself. So help me, we even had Go-Go dancers once.

Inherent in the whole fiasco was yet another serious error. We (somebody!) should have seen that Malka and Joso were not ready to star in a network television series—especially in that time slot. Whether they ever could be is another matter; they were not then. Knowing the vagaries of television, knowing the demands it makes on artists, knowing the built-in restrictions dictated by the economics (never enough rehearsal time, never ideal conditions), knowing how much experience counts in getting polished performances—knowing all this it's incredible that any of us could have been so foolish as to think you could take two coffee house and concert hall entertainers (however good in their milieu) and expect them to grasp, to adapt to, to discipline themselves to, to conquer all the problems that can engulf anyone thrust into the centre of a prime-time, sponsored, network television show week after week.

There was, to start with, an almost complete lack of communication between "us" and "them."[1] At first, Joso wanted to say almost nothing; could, in fact, say almost nothing in English. His beautiful partner, on the other hand, always had plenty to say and a compulsion to say it. There was, however, a sizable gulf between what she wanted to say and what Mark as producer or I as writer thought she should say. Arguments were not infrequent.

On the question of talking, Mark and I disagreed. He felt we should "protect" them, give them less and less to say, perhaps even consider adding a "host" who would introduce songs or guests. I argued that to do this was to take the show away from Malka and Joso. I felt we must stay with them, somehow muddle through the problem of their speech difficulties. I even suggested that Joso should take a crash course in English. Mark agreed and urged Joso to do so, but despite occasional promises that he would, he never got around to it.

Probably, too, in my zeal to make Malka more "acceptable" to the audience, I wrote the wrong things for her to say. Whatever the cause or combination of causes, she seemed to come off on the air as very haughty and cold whenever she spoke. Nor, it developed, was Malka particularly effective as a solo performer. She was best in combination with Joso; the metallic quality of her voice blended adequately with Joso's warmer one, but alone her singing sounded rather stark. Then, there was the matter of Malka's temperament, life-sized and ever-ready. In meetings she was outspoken (though not notably constructive) in her criticism of every aspect of the show—from costume design to script to staging.

Before the series started, she persuaded Joso, whose hairline was receding, that he should wear a hair piece. Poor Joso went whole hog—he got one so full and fluffy that he looked like a poor imitation of a shaggy teenager. It took some high-pressure salesmanship (not by me, thank goodness) to convince him he should get one a little more suited to his age and type. Malka, a strong-willed woman, domi-

---

[1] You really haven't lived until you've tried taking down over the telephone the lyrics to a song in Russian, Jugoslavian or Italian from Joso and then writing them, phonetically, into an English script.

Neither the picture nor the nose-scratching was posed. Juliette and Barris were absorbed in listening to a song. In four years of working together we did a lot of listening and a lot of nose-scratching.

Master musician Artie Shaw talked about his career and a fine group of Toronto musicians illustrated it on this segment of "Music Makers." Below, an early edition of "Front Page Challenge," with Don Ameche in the guest seat.

With actress Jayne Mansfield and her pet chihuahua. On camera the dog snapped at me, I blew cigaret smoke at him—and received angry letters from both dog lovers and cigaret haters.

Actor Don Murray (centre) and his producer, Walter Wood, were guests on my CFTO-TV program.

At Timmins, Ontario, with Conrad Lavigne, owner of CFCL-TV.

nated her mild-mannered partner. (They were both married, but not to each other.) One day, Mark and I ran into Joso and invited him to join us for a drink. He came with us but would have only a soft drink. He pointed to his stomach and said, "Ulcer." In response to our surprise at this news, he explained in his halting English: "You work with Malka, you have ulcer." No doubt, Malka's own insecurity about the show, her growing realization that it wasn't working, helped make her irritable and unco-operative.

After the second show (but not as a result of it) they were booked to appear on the Johnny Carson Show in New York. Everyone was happy for them and, to be honest, felt the interest of such a show in them tended to confirm our own shrewdness in starring them in our series. They returned triumphant. Their New York agent talked of big things—a return appearance with Carson, a guest shot with Como, and so on. And, as if she needed it, Malka came back with an extra supply of "chutzpah" in her personality.[1]

Malka became increasingly difficult. The script, page by page, was "terrible." Any suggestion from the director was dismissed. In one song, it was suggested Joso should place his hand on Malka's arm, a mild enough indication of affection. "No," Malka proclaimed imperiously, "Joso never touches me." A line in an introduction to a guest was rejected out of hand. "I won't say I'm delighted. I'm not delighted."

That week, we were to video-tape our show in a Yorkville coffee house. It was a harrowing day, due largely to Malka's moodiness. Andy Body, our choreographer and stager, complimented her, quite sincerely, in her appearance. "You look gorgeous," he said. "I know," she replied icily. At one point during a rehearsal immediately preceding the taping, Malka took issue with Mark over some point of direction. Mark, in the truck control-room on Yorkville Street, politely suggested through the studio director that if something was bothering Malka it could be discussed quietly. The studio director discreetly whispered this message to Malka. "There is nothing to discuss," she bellowed, in front of the invited audience. "He knows what I want. Let him do it."

---

[1] "Chutzpah," a Yiddish word meaning nerve or gall, has also been defined as that quality which allows a man to murder his parents and then plead for mercy on the grounds that he is an orphan.

For one brief outdoor shot, Malka complained about the cold, and an evening coat was hastily located. She refused to wear it, because it looked "awful." Somehow, we got through the taping. It was not a very good show. That it was not considerably worse can be attributed in more or less equal parts to Mark Warren's patience and the crew's skill.

So it went, from week to worry-laden week. The communication disintegrated, belief in the show slipped away, compromise increased. Press critics carped, sponsors looked on in stony silence, network brass viewed with alarm, Mark worried, I steamed. And we all compromised. Instead of the Russian dancers or Spanish guitarists we had all believed an audience somewhere out there was waiting to see, we substituted Shirley Harmer, Catherine McKinnon, a Mexican group gone Las Vegas, Malka and Joso trying to sing Scarlet Ribbons—anything, anything in a frantic attempt to bribe the at first apathetic but by now hostile (and predominantly WASP) audience that the show following hockey is heir to. Of the scores (or was it hundreds?) of acts we had auditioned, which were to bear out our original premise that there was, indeed a third force in Canada, I don't think we used more than three or four.

In the beginning, I had argued strongly in favor of having a studio audience, even though our show (after the first three weeks) was to be done in the cramped quarters of the Pierce-Arrow Showroom. I felt that, since Malka and Joso were predominantly coffee house performers, the presence of a live studio audience would make them more comfortable, elicit from them more natural performances. Somewhat reluctantly, as is usually the case with producers who must use every square foot of space efficiently, Mark agreed to the studio audience. But after a few weeks, it was tossed out. The show was "changing" and we needed more room for bigger sets and more elaborate productions. So, added to all the rest of the sham, Malka and Joso had to pretend they were entertaining people in a studio, to smile and say "thank you" in response to recorded applause. In the end it didn't really matter whether we had a studio audience or not. We were rapidly losing the home audience, the one that really counts in television.

Once happily confident of the show's chances for success,

we were distinctly uneasy by the fifth or sixth week. Also by this time my own dealings with Malka (but not particularly with Joso) had reached the strained state, followed soon by the hopeless state, where one no longer bothers to argue but accepts things as they are. After several stormy script-reading sessions, I concluded it was best for me not to be present when Malka went over the script with Mark. When he asked for rewrites, I did them—even if I disagreed —simply to avoid more unpleasant scenes. I had, in effect, given up on the show.

When a program is on a thirteen-week contract, the eighth and ninth weeks are considered critical. Traditionally, a decision is made by the ninth week as to whether the option will be picked up or not. If not, the show dies at the end of thirteen weeks. But by the eighth week I had already decided that I did not want to continue with it beyond the thirteen, come what may. I so informed Mark Warren, who was then in the process of trying to convince his superiors to keep the show on past the thirteen weeks. A week later he learned he had lost the battle. A World of Music was to be dropped and he was assigned to prepare its replacement. The replacement show was called "In Person" and it ran for the remainder of that season (twenty-six weeks) plus another full thirty-nine-week season. Malka and Joso returned to coffee houses and concerts. They subsequently broke up as a team, but both continued to work separately.

Should A World of Music have been dropped? Was the CBC right in taking it off the air? The alternatives were two: continue it in the face of audience and sponsor resistance; or move it to another time slot, where it might be less vulnerable to such pressures. The latter suggestion merits some examination. The initial error in judgment (and I had a part in it, however small) was in putting A World of Music on in the post-hockey spot. From this error stemmed the larger one of changing its concept, making compromises to appease that particular audience.

The same show (the original idea, that is) in another spot —say at six or seven on a Sunday evening—might well have succeeded. It might well have reached and pleased the audience for whom it was supposedly created. True, it would have had to live on a smaller budget, with no "name" guests, but we never got many of them, anyway. An earlier show, "Rhapsody," featuring international music, had done quite well, in the days when there weren't as many "New Canadians" or as many television viewers. It was unsponsored and therefore a money-loser to the CBC, but it was not subjected to the pressures of sponsorship, nor to the nervous scrutiny of a network trying to please the biggest possible audience. Without those obstacles, it went quietly along its unpretentious way, pleasing those people who were interested and not annoying those who wanted something entirely different after a hectic hockey game.

But to have moved the hybrid, compromise-ridden program that A World of Music had become into an early Sunday evening spot would probably have been as fruitless. For this show, hacked at and hammered shapeless to fit the square peg, would almost as surely have failed, with its unblendable mixture of Korean Kittens (that's an act, honest) and Las Vegas Mexicans, to appeal to that third force of Canadians we originally said we were trying to reach. By trying to appease the larger audience, we had lost what might have pleased the smaller one.

Somewhere in the dusty mountain of broadcast acts, Royal commission reports and parliamentary debates there is supposed to be a stated theory about public broadcasting in Canada—something about the responsibility for providing programs for a great diversity of tastes, rather than trying to make every show appeal to the greatest possible number of viewers.

In the case of A World of Music, we all of us lost sight of that obligation and carved out our own failure as surely as if we had chopped off the hands of a student pianist. Maybe Malka and Joso were the wrong people for that program, but we'll never know, because "that program" never got on the air.

The No-Star System

Have you ever heard the story of Wayne and Shuster's first trip to Hollywood? This was long before Ed Sullivan discovered them, thus giving Canadians a hint that maybe our leading (our only!) comedy team was good. It happened in the late 1950s, when Johnny Wayne and Frank Shuster were veterans of CBC radio, household names in a country where names seldom seem to matter. They had made the transition from radio to television and were doing their own regular network television show on the CBC.

A bid came from Hollywood. The Rosemary Clooney Show, then on NBC, wanted Wayne and Shuster to appear as guests on a program. Word had filtered down—these were the CBC's top comedians, so inviting them to appear on an American TV variety show made sense. Since this would be their first visit to Hollywood, Johnny and Frank decided to take their wives along and make it a combined business-and-pleasure trip.

When the foursome arrived in Los Angeles, the red carpet was out. They were met by a limousine, complete with network flunky to do the bowing and scraping. All the necessary arrangements had been made. A shopping and sight-seeing tour had been planned for Mrs. Wayne and Mrs. Shuster, to help make their stay a happy one. Hotel accommodations, naturally, were of the best. Wayne and Shuster were driven to the studio at the appointed time for the first rehearsal. Each was ushered to a dressing room, with a star on its door and his name neatly printed inside the star. Each was handed a Morocco-bound script of the program, with his name embossed in gold lettering on the cover.

In short, Wayne and Shuster were considered to be and

treated as stars. Their short stay in Hollywood was an altogether successful one. The program went well, they were paid a generous sum of money, they had been treated royally, and they left after receiving glowing words of praise and expressions of gratitude from the NBC people. Almost without benefit of aircraft, they flew back to Toronto, where they were to begin rehearsals almost immediately for their next CBC show. When they arrived at the CBC studio for the first rehearsal, the commissionaire wouldn't allow them to park on the CBC lot.

I relate this story not only because of its ironic twist, not merely because it illustrates vividly the contrast between American and Canadian attitudes toward stars. I relate it precisely because it is not unique. It has nothing particularly to do with the ignorance or even impudence of a commissionaire. It has much more to do with a CBC and Canadian philosophy (or lack of one) about stars.

There are, of course, other examples. In 1960, I was invited to be a guest on Showtime, at that time a long-running CBC Sunday evening television series. Its star (although his contract read "host") was Bob Goulet. When I arrived at the Pierce-Arrow Showroom on Sunday afternoon for rehearsal, I decided I'd drop into Bob's dressing room to say hello.

As I mentioned earlier, the studio has two main dressing rooms—one for men, one for women. In addition, there is a small dressing room, at the other end of the studio, sometimes used for guest performers, occasionaly for a resident artist. I assumed that on this show it would be Goulet's. But when I went there, I found only Len Casey, who was then producing the program. I said that I thought Bob would be there. "No," he said. "There are no stars on this show. I use this room as a kind of office."

Later that day I learned from Goulet that he had just returned from New York, where he had auditioned for a leading role in Camelot—and won it. He was good enough to have been chosen, over a good many competitors, by Alan Jay Lerner, Frederick Loewe and Moss Hart. But he was no star to Casey.

In its ten years on the air, the Juliette Show was forever tripping over budgetary limitations that reflected the CBC's reluctance to recognize Julie's stardom. There was rarely enough money to make gowns for her (frequently they were gowns "in stock" that were remodelled for her), the money available for guest performers invariably restricted the calibre of guests who could realistically be invited, the show was always treated as a "little" show, it was not unusual for a producer to be taken off the show temporarily—to do some "important" program.

Juliette herself was reasonably well paid, by Canadian show business standards. By her last season, she was making one thousand to twelve hundred dollars a week. But she alone knows how bitterly she had to fight to get that much— and remember that was after she'd had her own program for a decade. But it isn't only the money; it's the attitude— hard, perhaps, to define, harder still to understand.

Example: During the run of Flashback (whether you liked it or not, a successful, popular show that ran for six years) a manufacturer of television sets decided to make up an ad showing one of its products with some familiar faces inside the TV screen. The manufacturer (through his advertising agency) decided to use the Flashback personalities—panelists Elwy Yost, Maggie Morris and Allan Manings, and moderator Bill Walker. The ad appeared in a number of magazines, urging people to buy that particular make of TV set for a good, clear picture, et cetera. One of the panelists, Allan Manings, was furious that this should be done without their —or, at least, his—consent. First of all, this kind of advertising, suggestive of a testimonial, is a potential source of income for anybody working in show business.

One reason why an advertiser is expected to pay for such use of a performer's picture is that its use might well boomerang on the performer. In future, some rival TV set manufacturer could well reject Allan Manings or one of the others for a projected program that the manufacturer was going to sponsor, on the grounds that the personality was already "identified" with a rival product. Yet the manufacturer in question never bothered to seek permission from the performers. The photograph was simply obtained from the CBC. And the CBC granted permission to use the photograph without so much as consulting the performers concerned. The photograph, after all, was the property of the

CBC. So, presumably, are the performers.[1] The whole incident suggests that the CBC no-star policy is contagious—it can be caught by others in the television business: sponsors, advertising agencies. Worse still, it can be caught by the public.

I remember a conversation on a train one time some years ago, when I was going to Moncton to speak at a dinner. A club-car companion and I were discussing television people. He, it turned out, thought that Wayne and Shuster were great. "What do they do?" he asked me at one point.

I said I didn't understand what he meant. "I mean, what do they do? I know that you write for a newspaper besides doing your TV show. What do they do?"

It was difficult to explain to him that what they "do" is their television work. It was not intended as a slur on the comedians. The man simply didn't recognize Canadian television as a career. He assumed Wayne and Shuster had some other source of income. I'm sure the same man had no similar misconceptions about Jackie Gleason or Dinah Shore or Perry Como. They were stars. But Canadian stars? It never occurred to him. It may seem unfair to blame the CBC for the famous Canadian inferiority complex. That there is more to it than the CBC's determination to deflate show business egos is clear.

Johnny Wayne tells (without cheer) of being introduced to a man at a party. This was when Johnny and Frank were appearing with great frequency on the Ed Sullivan Show.[2] When the man met Johnny he could hardly contain his enthusiasm. He was one of their greatest fans, he never missed them on TV, et cetera, et cetera. When would they be on again, how soon, he could hardly wait. "Well, as a matter of fact," said Johnny, "we're in the midst of rehearsing our next CBC show. It will be on the air in a couple of weeks." "Oh, no," said the man. "I never watch the CBC. I mean when will you be on the Sullivan show again?"

It's all too true, I'm afraid, that so many Canadians look outside the country for stamps of approval. We do not recog-

---

[1] It may be sheer coincidence that Manings was eased out of the program after this dispute, although the series continued for several more seasons.
[2] As of this writing, Sullivan has used Wayne and Shuster more often than any other act in his 21 years of running a TV show. They have appeared more than 50 times.

nize that Wayne and Shuster are good until Sullivan tells us so. We do not admire Bob Goulet or Lorne Greene or Paul Anka or Christopher Plummer until such artists win the approval of other, non-Canadian judges. The measure of Canadian merit seems always to be checked on an American yardstick of success. In show business, at least, the Canadian public's attitude suggests that you don't arrive until you've left. Larry Mann, the actor who finally reluctantly moved to Hollywood in 1965, put it this way to me in an interview in 1964: "You can be a full-time garbage collector in Toronto and you'll be accepted as such. Nobody says, 'If he were any good he'd be collecting garbage in New York.' Or you can be a successful doctor or lawyer or accountant. You're not expected to prove how good you are by moving away to practice medicine or law or accounting in Hollywood or London."

I'm not suggesting the CBC is entirely to blame for all this. No doubt it existed before the CBC did. But no one is in a better position than the CBC to do something about fostering recognition of Canadian artistic achievement; nobody is better equipped to "sell" Canadian stars to the Canadian public.

That the CBC does nothing of the sort is abundantly clear. Take a look at a partial list of musical and variety shows put on by the CBC in its years in television: The Big Revue, After Hours, Four for the Show, Eleven Thirty Friday, Showtime, On Stage, Music Hall, Holiday Ranch, PM Party, Music Makers, Music '60, World of Music (also A World of Music), Nightcap, Country Hoedown, Swing Easy, Swing Gently, Saturday Date, Country Club, Come Fly with Me, Parade, Moonlight Bay, A la Carte. Plus probably a dozen more whose titles I can't come up with. (Against this, just a handful of shows named for people: Wayne and Shuster, Juliette, Tommy Hunter, Joan Fairfax.)

But look at that sickly list of titles. Nameless, faceless, bloodless titles, all of them. Starring nobody, featuring nobody, presenting nobody, spotlighting nobody. After a while the titles melt into each other in one's memory—even when you've been associated with some of them.

This is no accident. The CBC has always been uneasy about proclaiming anyone as a "star." I don't suggest this is done out of spite, although, of course, money has something to do with it. A "star" is more likely to demand a raise, a personality around whom a show is built might move on to the United States. Better, far simpler, to create shows which, should they succeed, could be retained (with the same flat title) even though this Goulet or that Harmer might leave.

But it doesn't work out quite that easily. At least in the area of variety entertainment, what television is all about is people, not show titles; personalities, not electronic magic; human beings, not elaborate sets. Television is an intimate medium. It works best when somebody in front of the camera makes contact with the viewer in his living room. It's Arthur Godfrey or Johnny Carson or Dean Martin or Juliette that attracts the viewer—not some clever title or brilliant camera angle.

I have yet to hear anyone (apart from people in the business) say, "Gee, that was a great set on the Carol Burnett Show." What they say is, "Hey, did you catch Steve Lawrence on the Sullivan Show?" I have never heard anyone comment on the set in front of which Ella Fitzgerald sang, or the number of strings in the band on Andy Williams' show.

Sure, you need all the trappings. You need sets, costumes, orchestrations, dancers, visual novelties, smooth production, intelligent direction—all the elements that go into making a show. But all of these should be used like a supporting cast, all should be made to serve the program—whose function it must be to showcase the star, to present a human being, a personality, a gifted artist who is the *raison d'être* of the show—not to detract or distract, not to clutter up, surely not to cover up a lack of faith in that star.

Let's suppose that someone argues (and someone is sure to) that we simply don't have stars of that magnitude, with a very few exceptions. *If* that's true, does it necessarily suggest some lack in our personality as a people, some inability to produce gifted artists, some inherent flaw in our national character that makes Canadians incapable of becoming successful, outstanding, dynamic, appealing creative artists?

Nonsense. That conclusion would be an insult to such actors and actresses as Christopher Plummer, Kate Reid,

Douglas Rain, William Hutt, Bruno Gerussi, Barbara Hamilton, William Shatner, Lorne Greene, Lou Jacobi, Frances Hyland, Lloyd Bochner, John Vernon, Martha Henry, John Colicos, Gordon Pinsent, Donald Davis, and the late John Drainie; to such singers as Lois Marshall, Teresa Stratas, Jon Vickers, Jan Rubes; to such musicians as Glenn Gould, Oscar Peterson, Percy Faith; to such entertainers in the popular field as Robert Goulet, Paul Anka, Don Francks, Rich Little, Gisele Mackenzie, Alan Young; to such diverse writers as Mazo de la Roche, W. O. Mitchell, Mordecai Richler, Len Peterson, Charles Israel, Arthur Hailey, Brian Moore, Joseph Schull; to such assorted artists as Celia Franca, Mavor Moore, Gratien Gelinas, Lois Smith, Monique Leyrac, Jack Creley, Gordon Lightfoot and many more.[1]

All right, let us accept the argument that this national inferiority complex is not the CBC's fault. We are still a young country, culturally; we live in the huge shadow of the United States and have long ago fallen into the habit of comparing, consciously or not, our attempts with theirs; we have neither the tradition of show business (burlesque, vaudeville, night clubs, theatres) that they have nor the population to support a full-scale entertainment industry on their scale without public financial support; further, we, like all human beings, tend to be more impressed with the imported, the exotic, than with the home-grown product—be it wine, magazines, fashions, football players, films or fun.

Accept all of that. It still does not absolve the CBC of the responsibility for doing something about it. Instead, the Corporation, reflecting the public, falls into this same trap. When there was more television drama being done in this country, the CBC many times passed over thoroughly capable Canadian actors (and writers) in favor of imported ones. Their defense, of course, was that the sponsor or the public demanded well-known names. But all too often, the imported actors were not even that. Good actors they may have been—I don't dispute that—but they weren't box office names. The CBC, like the public and the sponsors, simply had not enough faith in the Canadian actors available.

[1] I have purposely left out two groups: the Bea Lillie-Norma Shearer-Maria Dressler-Glenn Ford stars who did not really develop their talents here; and the television producers, directors and writers, who will receive separate attention later.

In light entertainment, the name trap has been even bigger. The CBC felt proud, I recall, that Sammy Davis Jr. was once persuaded to journey to Toronto to star in a half-hour program in the "Parade" series. I am a great admirer of Sammy's, but I couldn't join in the cheering. Who couldn't do a TV one-man show with Sammy Davis? What genius does that take? What great achievement does it represent? What credit reflects on the CBC for this undertaking?

The same thing has happened again and again at the CBC —Harry Belafonte, Duke Ellington, Mel Torme, Patrice Munsel, Nat Cole, Juliette Prowse, Pete Seeger, Mort Sahl, Mitch Miller, Victor Borge, and so on. I have respect and admiration for most of these artists and I certainly do not believe our borders should be closed to them. But neither do I believe they should displace the bulk of Canadian artists in the television industry here—because the CBC and the sponsors lack confidence in them.

Because that's really what it's all about—lack of confidence in the potential of this country, in the people who should and can attain artistic or creative heights that will help to counterbalance that tired old inferiority complex we keep hearing about; worse still, a lack of confidence in their own network, their own concept of public broadcasting; worst of all, a lack of confidence in their own ability to find, develop and present proudly Canadian stars, a shakiness in their own self-confidence. Let us admit this lack of self-confidence is not exclusively Canadian—particularly in the world of entertainment. No producer, entrepreneur, promoter, packager or creator of any kind of show anywhere knows for certain that his project will succeed. If anyone had found a magic, foolproof formula, there would be no flops of any kind.

I am convinced this is as true in Hollywood as it is here. As an ironic example, you have only to examine Hollywood's current, almost mystical faith in Canadians. For the past few years, any writer or director who was from Canada found a more receptive atmosphere than if he'd been from, say, Australia or Chicago. This was mostly because a number of Canadians (Peppiatt and Aylesworth, Norman Jewison, Bernard Slade) had registered favorably. But it makes no more sense to assume that any Canadian journeying to Hollywood is a genius than to assume that because one is from Australia (or Jugoslavia or Canada) he is necessarily inferior, inadequate or untalented.

The point is that nobody knows for sure. Deep in his soul, the most persuasive, positive-sounding, supersalesman of a producer confesses to himself: "I'm not sure; I wish I were sure." But he can't be. Nobody can. So he weighs the possibilities, the risks, the odds—and takes a chance. A lot of producers and networks and studios and backers take a lot of chances. And a lot of those gambles fail. But some succeed. As the producer (or promoter or network) gains experience, his batting average may improve. But he has to start by taking chances—and he has to continue taking them.

Now, what is the CBC's record in this regard? Not all that impressive, I'm afraid. Naturally, lip service is paid to the importance of "developing" talent, but over the years the approach hasn't been especially practical.

Some years back, the CBC produced such series as "Pick the Stars" and "Talent Caravan." The idea was to seek out new talent and present this talent to Canadian audiences. It was on Pick the Stars that such newcomers as Paul Anka and Rich Little got their first national television exposure. That these two entertainers have done rather well since those days, however, is no credit to the CBC. They had to struggle on their own, mostly outside the CBC, mostly outside Canada, for recognition. Talent Caravan spent much money and effort in unearthing talented hopefuls from coast to coast. So what? Each week a winner was declared, then a "grand" winner of the season. Still, so what? A handful of them were subsequently brought to Toronto to appear as guests on national variety shows.

More often than not, the pressure of this big leap proved too much for the budding performer. He fumbled nervously through his one big chance at bat and failed to deliver adequately. The wise men shook their heads sadly, and the youngster went back to Moose Jaw or Moncton, never again to be summoned by the CBC in Toronto.

Would it not make more sense for such promising young performers to be given an opportunity by the CBC to develop their talent in their local regions, under CBC guidance, to gain the experience and poise necessary for success, and *then* be exposed on national television? But no such machinery existed. The "winners" got one chance, often proved understandably unequal to the task and were quietly dropped.

In a way, much the same thing has been done on a national basis. The CBC decides to feature (never "star") some talented young performer in a series. Sometimes the performer isn't quite ready; sometimes the network loses faith in the idea after giving the show only a few weeks to find its level or style. Think back to a program called "Come Fly With Me" and a young man named Shane Rimmer. Or to Jack Duffy and his series, "Here's Duffy." Or to Tommy Ambrose. Or to Don Francks and Patti Lewis and a show titled "Country Club." Or to Peppiatt and Aylesworth, or Allan Blye, or Malka and Joso. The CBC plunged them into the national television spotlight, then lost confidence in them and dumped them.

This is a particularly serious business in Canada, much more so than in the United States. Below the border, an entertainer who gets national exposure on television for a season and then has his show dropped can usually make a comfortable living by working in night clubs or theatres, keeping his career alive until the next television (or movie) break comes along. As examples, consider George Gobel, Pat Boone, Polly Bergen, Nancy Ames or John Davidson.

But what does the Canadian do? Once his TV program has been chopped, his name is a dirty word around television for some time to come. There aren't enough programs for him to do guest appearances on, even if he were welcome. There aren't enough night clubs or theatres to keep him working. Ask Jack Duffy or Don Francks or Cliff McKay or Tommy Ambrose about the lean years that *followed* their great "opportunity" on the CBC.

And far too often the reason is the same: because the new program isn't an overnight smash hit, or because the performer fails to acquire immediately the polish and professionalism required, the CBC loses its confidence, picks up its marbles and runs to hide, leaving a dazed, wounded performer to fend for himself. Of all people, of all institutions, of all media of communication the CBC is the one that should reflect some measure of confidence in the ability of Canadian artists to prove themselves. And if that means taking a chance, then the CBC should be willing to take that chance. More important, the CBC should then stick to its decision and give the show or the performer a reasonable time to win public acceptance.

Confidence is still the hallmark of a successful entrepreneur—confidence in the young artist he has chosen and in his own judgment in making that choice. An Otto Preminger has confidence in an unknown like Jean Seberg and casts her as St. Joan. His gamble doesn't pay off at first, but in time she develops into an acceptable screen actress— proving that Preminger was right in sensing her potential. A Ray Stark bets a bundle of money on Barbra Streisand in *Funny Girl*—and launches a fantastically successful career. A network official at CBS decides to try the Smothers Brothers in a show of their own. A producing team (Schlatter and Friendly) sells hard to convince NBC to try Rowan and Martin's "Laugh-In." A Colonel Parker believes in a young entertainer named Elvis Presley. A Polish film director named Roman Polanski sees something in Mia Farrow that nobody else has detected and casts her in *Rosemary's Baby*. A Mike Nichols decides that an unknown named Dustin Hoffman is just right as The Graduate. A recording company takes a fling on an unheard of singing group called The Beatles. Somebody at the Westinghouse network decides to give Merv Griffin a chance at a ninety-minute talk-and-variety show. A Warren Beatty is convinced there is a successful movie in *Bonnie and Clyde*. A Moss Hart decides the handsome Canadian singer named Bob Goulet is the man to play Lancelot in *Camelot*. An Elia Kazan takes a chance on an unknown Marlon Brando to play Stanley Kowalski.

There are a thousand stories like it—and a hundred thousand that didn't work out. But without the hundred thousand individual gambles there wouldn't be the thousand successes. Without the faith, the risk, the payoff is impossible. This is why I argue against the timidity of the CBC, against the let's-play-it-safe attitude, against the fear to show faith in the ability of Canadian entertainers to become stars. Even if there is some validity to the danger that CBC-created stars might become "monsters" and eventually defect to the United States, it's not reason enough for the CBC's no-star philosophy. Too many of our talented people have left anyway—very often out of frustration—and gone on to prove their ability outside Canada.

Whenever that happens, the CBC is berated for letting them get away. Would it not be better to build stars, to encourage them, even at the risk that they might leave? At least, then those who left would reflect some credit on the CBC and on Canada. It could then be said that Canada or the CBC produced that star. As it is now, most Americans (or Europeans) are hardly aware that Goulet, Greene or Plummer are Canadians. If they leave here as stars and become bigger international stars, at least Canada and the CBC could legitimately take some of the credit. And our famous inferiority complex might start to disappear.

What we have now—the no-star system—has worked only in the sense that it has produced no stars (Juliette and Wayne and Shuster excepted). Certainly nobody in the United States or Britain is the least bit interested in buying or showing no-star programs with innocuous titles like "On Stage" or "In Person." People in Canada have trouble enough remembering those titles or what they represented a year after the shows have died. Like it or not, the CBC is in the people business. The sooner it recognizes that fact and faces up to the need to take chances and have a little faith, the sooner it will begin to make a better impression both inside and outside Canada.

The Games Producers Play

One of the traps the CBC has dug for itself is related to its no-star policy. Having taken the position that no performer is big or important enough to be in command of "his" show, the Corporation must then put its money on somebody else, somebody who is responsible for the program, somebody whom the performer must regard as his "boss."

That person, quite logically, is the producer. In the case of the CBC, he is usually a producer-director. In U.S. network television, to a much greater degree, the two functions are separated: virtually all network programs have one man as producer, another as director. Often, too, there is an executive producer, but his is essentially a supervisory role.

It might be useful here to take a moment to explain the nature of the two jobs as they relate to television. The difference between the producer and director is roughly the same as the difference between a strategist and a tactician. The producer is in overall charge of the program. He organizes it, sets into motion every aspect of it—from writing to casting, to design of costumes and sets, to apportioning the budget, to planning the working schedule. The director's job is to execute the producer's plan. Once in the studio (or even a rehearsal hall) the director is pretty much in charge. He plans and carries out the shooting of the show and the producer will not interfere with him unless he feels that the director is doing something seriously wrong.

In Canadian television, these functions have usually been combined. That is, one man acts as producer, planning the show. Then he changes hats, becomes the director and carries out his own strategy. The chief reason for this system at the CBC is an economic one. It is simply less expensive to have one man perform two jobs, and the CBC is ever aware of the need to keep costs down wherever possible.

The system places a heavy burden on the producer-director. It could be argued that he is given too much responsibility. Some of these men are better producers than directors, some vice versa. It is not every producer who has the "eye" for direction, the sensitivity, the special skill for handling people, or the ability to remain calm under the pressures of a control room. Nor is it every good director who has the organizational ability required of a good producer. But probably the most serious defect of the one-man system is that one man means one viewpoint. The producer-director can't very well argue with himself. I think the CBC is aware of these problems and in recent years has begun moving—however slowly—in the direction of separating the two jobs.

One further digression is necessary. I said earlier that in U.S. television (and in theatre and films) the producer is in charge. That does not always apply when you are dealing with big stars. No producer is in command of Johnny Carson, Dean Martin, Ed Sullivan, Red Skelton or other such stars. More often than not, the stars hire their producers and tend to dominate them. And even where the producer is nominally in charge he is still subject to the wishes of the star. This, of course, is also true when you speak of Frank Sinatra or Marlon Brando in the film world, or of Ethel Merman or Henry Fonda in the theatre. They are "bigger" than their producers or directors and not very much about their productions will be done without their approval. But at the CBC it's different; with very few exceptions (and again Wayne and Shuster and Juliette come to mind) the producer-director—or, in those cases where the job has been split, the producer—is in command.

(A producer-director naturally has jurisdiction over the writing on a program too, but his power can become awesome when he is also involved as a writer on the same show. I once had the experience of working, for ten weeks, as co-writer of the Joan Fairfax Show. The other writer was Len Casey, who was also producer-director. The system we used was simple enough on the surface. One week, I wrote the script subject to his approval; the other week, he wrote it, subject to his own approval. Casey the writer turned his script over to Casey the producer who then handed it over to Casey the director; all three of them got along famously. But when it was my week to write, both producer Casey and director Casey felt entitled to take liberties with my script. When I found that drastic changes were being made regularly with my scripts—without any discussion with me—I asked for and got a release from my contract.)

The trap I referred to at the beginning of this chapter is that the CBC has avoided creating one kind of "monster" (the star) at the expense of creating another kind—the producer-director. After all, the producer-director is just as capable as the star of demanding better terms, greater money, more freedom in working, bigger shows to do. And he tries to get them by brandishing the same weapon—the threat that he will leave Canada and go to Hollywood, New York or London.

By trying to keep the performer off a pedestal, the CBC has made it easier for the producer to occupy it. And what has been gained? Are the producers any more "loyal" to the CBC? Are they any less likely to defect to American television? Hardly. Among the variety producer-directors who have gone from the CBC to greener fields are Norman Jewison, Stan Harris, Bill Davis, Norman Sedawie, Harvey Hart, Stan Jacobson and Mark Warren. Then, there have been drama producers like Daryl Duke, Silvio Narizzano, Eric Till, Ted Kotcheff, George McCowan, Arthur Hiller and David Greene—all gone from the CBC to England or the United States. Of those who are still here, most have or are trying to get agents in the U.S. to represent them; they store up kinescopes of their shows to demonstrate their work; they bide their time here, waiting for just the right offer from outside Canada.

I am not, incidentally, among those who consider such people to be "traitors," be they actors, singers, producers or writers. I think it is natural that any artist should feel a compulsion to seek the widest recognition of his talents, the greatest audience for his message, the biggest reward for his efforts. Artists from other countries leave their homelands to seek just such enlargement of their careers. I see no good reason why Canadians should be expected to behave differently, particularly when, for whatever combination of reasons, we in Canada seem unwilling or unable to provide a challenging enough or rewarding enough atmosphere for the artist.

What I am saying is that it seems foolish to me for the CBC to calculatedly stifle the ambitions or egos of Canadian actors or performers while at the same time treating its producer-directors as stars. It's interesting, incidentally, that this is reflected in the press coverage of Canadian television news and gossip—and having spent some fifteen years working on the entertainment pages of two metropolitan newspapers, I know a little bit about it. The comings and goings, the actions and reactions, the successes and failures, the peccadillos or pronouncements of Canadian producers and directors are generally more widely reported than the activities of performers.

Who knows through the papers that Tommy Hunter has gone to Nashville to record? That Bill Walker is appearing in a musical comedy in Winnipeg? That Al Hamel has done a pilot in Hollywood? That Gordon Pinsent has landed a movie? That Juliette drew a crowd of two thousand at Sydney? That Sandra O'Neill starred in *Little Me* in Florida? That Mary Lou Collins is touring with Bob Hope?

But we know each time Ross McLean starts a new series. We read reams about Douglas Leiterman and Patrick Watson when they get into trouble with the CBC brass. We all know that Bob Jarvis was moving to New York to do a show for CBS. We know all about Maxene Samuels, lady producer of Seaway. We read of the arrivals and departures of Daryl Duke. We know about Norman Campbell's trip to New York to produce a Gilbert and Sullivan operetta. We know when Terry Kyne is doing a Nightcap program for a local New York station. We know all about Alan King and Warrendale or Dick Ballantine and Mr. Pearson. About Peter Reilly's switch from CBC to CTV and back again. About Stan Jacobson's move to Hollywood, or Mark Warren's. About Drew Crossan's assignment in Africa, and Franz Kraemer's latest special with Stravinsky, and Paddy Sampson's project with Harry Belafonte.

This sort of thing in the press has always struck me as

rather provincial, but it results partly from the CBC's practice of focusing on producers, of elevating them to star status, rather than the people in front of the cameras—the ones the public sees. Do you think New Yorkers or Californians give a damn when Dinah Shore and her producer split? Does anyone know or care that Ed Sullivan's producer is his son-in-law, Bob Precht? Can anyone outside the trade tell me who Joey Bishop's producer is, or Walter Cronkite's or Dean Martin's? Readers of Canadian newspapers and magazines know (or at least have ample opportunity to know) that Saul Ilson, a Canadian, was the producer of the Smothers Brothers Show and was succeeded by Allan Blye, another Canadian. Do you think readers in the United States know or care? Certainly not. They read instead about the Smothers Brothers, or about Jerry Lewis or Andy Williams or Eva Gabor.

(I can think of very few U.S. television "trade" stories that hit the news pages. One was the resignation from CBS of that network's news director, Fred Friendly, over the network's decision to air a rerun of I Love Lucy in preference to a Congressional hearing on the U.S. role in Vietnam. Another was the departure from the same network of James Aubrey, an executive who left in a cloud of scandal. Both were legitimate "hard" news stories and were treated accordingly. But nothing like the field day the press here had over the Seven Days blow-up, which was regarded by some large papers as too juicy an anti-CBC tidbit to be viewed in its proper perspective.)

None of this, by the way, is intended by me to belittle either the importance or the ability of CBC producer-directors. In the past dozen years, I have worked with a great many of them (mostly but not exclusively in light entertainment) and found them much like any other group of people—some are gifted, some less so, some are easy to work with, some stubborn, some well-organized, some old fashioned, some too "far out," some too far "in," some intelligent, some less so, some courageous, some too timid.

And I know too that to be a producer-director at the CBC, and probably elsewhere, requires a great deal of patience, fortitude, understanding and determination. That's just to be a producer-director—to be a good one requires still more skills and gifts. For the fact is that despite the credit on the screen, the producer very often does not have the freedom his responsibility implies. He is sometimes supervised too tightly, limited by budgets, pressured by time, hampered by inadequate facilities, frustrated by "brass" decisions made without his knowledge, ruled by considerations that have no relationship to the merits of a program, saddled with programs (or performers) he doesn't want, subjected to unfair appraisal of his work by unknowing critics.

Quite apart from monetary rewards—and they are usually greater in the United States than in Canada—it's no wonder that eventually so many producer-directors cross the border into the promised land, hoping that things will be better there. But the departure of a dozen Jewisons or Hillers doesn't change anything at the CBC. The system goes on; the producers may be different people, but the conditions under which they work (and consequently under which everyone else involved in a show works) remain the same.

This system and these conditions have a bearing on the degree of success that television programs can achieve. And so, of course, do the complexities of the medium. Television is a very complex business. Like the theatre and film, it requires the combined talents and energies of a great many artists and craftsmen. The difficult thing is to get all these people to work toward the same goal. It's an exhausted cliché of show business that "everyone wants a good show." Of course they do, but what kind of show? The trick is to get everyone to "see" the same show. And in television—far more so than in theatre or films—the time element is crucial.

The communication of ideas from one mind to another is no simple matter—ironically enough, not even in a medium of communication. The transferring of an idea from one person to another is like passing handfuls of water—every time you pass it along, you lose a little water. A writer may have an idea for a TV program. He explains it, verbally or on paper, to a producer. The producer likes it and decides to act on it. He passes it on to his production staff—designer, musical director, et cetera. Each of these men must then pass it on to their subordinates or associates. By the time the idea has been passed along a few times, what emerges may bear little or no resemblance to the original idea. The writer comes into the studio for rehearsal and wonders what happened. "That's not what I had in mind," he mutters dejectedly, but it's too late to do anything about it.

Add to this the independence of spirit of most creative people. They want not merely to carry out instructions, but to interpret, to apply their craft, to add something they feel will improve the idea. I have seen it happen often—musical arrangements that suggest a different mood than the one envisioned by the producer; costumes that look different than they did in the designer's sketch; sets too elaborate to be assembled or taken apart in the available time; direction that changes the meaning of dialogue.

Here's a more detailed example. One week on The Barris Beat we wrote a comedy sketch about four people playing bridge and gossiping. Their talk was about celebrities—each gossip claiming inside knowledge about this star or that. It was broadly exaggerated, of course, but comedy often is. Anyway, towards the end of the sketch one of the gossips was to start talking about me. "That fellow Barris," his lines went, "he doesn't get paid for appearing on TV. He works for the *Telegram*. He makes his living delivering papers." Just when the others in the sketch were voicing their rejection of this ridiculous theory, there was to be a knock at the door. When the door was opened it would reveal me—collecting for the *Telegram*.

The producer liked the sketch and it was decided we'd do it. At a production meeting, he outlined it briefly to the production staff—with each member taking notes as to the requirements of the comedy sketch.

On the day of the show, the time came to rehearse the sketch and Jewison (the producer-director) asked for the set for it to be put into place. In came an attractive wall, looking like the inside of a living room, with a door placed smack in the middle of it. But there was one slight problem: the door was merely painted on, it was not a "practical" door. Jewison called for the designer who explained that a real door would have ruined "the line" of his design and therefore he had decided on a false, painted door. The fact that the "blow" of the comedy sketch depended on the door opening didn't faze him a bit. His attitude was, "So, change the ending."

In time, he was persuaded to cut a door in his precious

wall. But the point is, he really felt the appearance of the set was more important than the content of the comedy sketch that was to be played in front of it. It's human enough that everyone connected with the production of a television show should feel its success depends on his particular contribution. In a way, this is true—the success depends on the combined contributions of all concerned.

But one of the greatest flaws in television—and particularly in Canadian television, where the producer is the "star"—is that too often the importance of the people in front of the cameras is minimized. The producer-director and his staff tend to form a bloc, which somehow excludes the performers.

Producers all too often delude themselves, believing that gimmickry, gadgetry, eye-popping sets and costumes, battalions of dancers, or twenty-four additional violins will make a show successful. If Frank Sinatra sings well or Bob Hope is funny, the set behind Sinatra or the color of Hope's jacket won't really matter. And if the performer is inadequate, not all the fancy trappings a producer or his aides can whip up will make him seem any better.

One of the games producers play is prerecording—that is, putting on audio tape the orchestral or vocal rendition (or both) of a song and then, on the air, having the singer who recorded the song stand in front of a camera and pretend to sing it, by trying to "mouth" the lyrics in synchronization with a playback of the tape. Sometimes, a song will be "band-tracked"—that is, the orchestra will be recorded but the singer will perform "live" to a playback of the band-track. In the early days of television, this was not allowed (because of some musicians' union objection) and producers had to be content with presenting all songs "live." I'm still not sure we weren't all better off then.

First, let's state the case for prerecording. Television studios don't often have the best acoustics, so it is usually possible to get a better sound "balance" by prerecording a song in a properly built recording studio. Thus there is less danger of a band drowning out a singer, or one section of the band being too loud in relation to another. Second, an orchestra takes up a fair bit of room in a TV studio. If you can have all your music prerecorded, you needn't lose the studio space to an orchestra when you are doing a show.

Third, it is far easier in production numbers that call for dancing or movement to "shoot" the number if you don't have to worry about keeping a microphone close enough to the singer or singers to pick up the sound, but still not visible to the home audience.

All these are sometimes valid arguments. But there is another side to the issue. No singer, I don't care how professional he may be, can look as convincing while pretending to sing as when he is actually singing. It is true, prerecording of musical numbers has been done in motion pictures for years, but it takes a great deal of time to do it perfectly—and time is a luxury rarely available in television.

I will concede that there are instances when prerecording is justified. But the trouble is that most producers will prerecord even when it isn't really necessary—merely because it is convenient for them. Never mind that the singer (the person whose bare face is out there on camera, the one being judged by the audience) looks foolish, or unsteady, or unreal; never mind that the singer now has to concentrate so much on lip-synchronization that he may look like an idiot, his facial expression bearing no relation to the meaning of the lyric he's pretending to sing. The producer prefers to "play it safe"—safe for him.

The prerecording practice is sometimes even carried to the ridiculous extreme of having singers on camera holding microphones, pretending to sing into them—yet the songs have been prerecorded. And there is no apparent reason—no movement is involved, the sound balance is not all that good, the band is on camera anyway. Too often I have seen performers sacrificed, not so much for the good of the show as because their wishes, their requirements, their comfort is not considered that important.

A young singer, perhaps not too experienced in television, will be brought into a studio to do a song in a show. The producer (now a director) will explain to the singer the camera cuts, the movements he wants her to make, and so on. The song will, of course, have been prerecorded by the singer. Now the singer—who really is on the show to *sing*—is not to sing; instead she has to concentrate on (a) certain prescribed movements she must make from this spot in the studio to that, at certain points in the song; (b) the playback she hears over the loudspeaker, so that her lips will move precisely to the tempo and phrasing of her prerecorded song; (c) where the cameras are, which one she must play to here, which one is on at the moment. What fraction of her concentration is still left unoccupied by such external considerations may be used to try to look as if she means the song she is pretending to sing.

The singer will run through the number, frequently being stopped and told to start over. Usually, this is so the director can correct or improve his shots—but everyone is too busy to bother telling her this. So she stands there, under the hot lights, going over it and over it, never being certain just what is wrong, rarely asked how *she* feels about it. The director, by now absorbed in directing cameras and checking lighting and worrying about a hundred technical details, has no time to direct the person on camera.

The time for the show comes. The performer, pretending to sing while mouthing lyrics, pretending to move naturally for no reason she understands, pretending to turn gracefully from this camera to that without knowing why she's supposed to do so, gets through the song. If she's lucky and very careful she will not have "blown" the lyrics—twice as obvious an error now that the prerecorded tape can give her mistakes away; if she's lucky, she will have remembered all the moves and smiles and turns. And if she's extremely lucky, the audience at home will think she's not too bad. That she could have been a lot better without all these pressures on her is something the audience will never know.

All this relates back to the system—a system in which there are no stars, in which Father Producer always knows best, in which the object is to do programs rather than to present real people. Quite naturally, the producer-director, trained in this philosophy, living under this system, becomes program-oriented rather than people-oriented. He comes to believe in the importance of sets, costumes, camera shooting, musical arranging, electronic devices, all those things called "production values"—often at the expense of the performers. He even knows, in time, that his worth as a producer-director is going to be judged within the CBC on the slickness of his shooting, on the beauty of the sets, on the inventiveness of his use of all the facilities—except the people on camera. And if the people in front of the cameras fail to make contact with the people in front of the television sets, the performers are judged to "lack" something; they may be dropped, but the producer-director will go on to another CBC non-people program.

I remember an incident in a show I was involved in. The director came into a production meeting one day all excited about a new gimmick he'd come across—some sort of sheets of artificial ice that could be laid down on a studio floor and were strong enough and smooth enough to skate on. He thought it would be great and felt very strongly that we should quickly buy or rent some of this artificial ice, so our show could be the first to make use of it on television. I asked him what—or who—would be presented on this ice. He was stuck for an answer; he simply hadn't thought about that—it was relatively unimportant in his mind. What did matter was being "first" with the latest gimmick.

Nor is this kind of thinking so unusual. We have all seen countless "spectaculars" shot in locations like the Toronto Islands or some beautiful park, with great long-shots that cover acres of ground, with some lonely little figure about the size of a fly speck on our home screens singing out as if she were standing three feet away from us. Or those equally ludicrous production numbers in which a dozen dancers (looking like a dozen fly specks) romp around energetically, washed in ever-changing swirls of psychedelic lighting, while a boy and girl try to look convincing as they mouth the prerecorded lyrics of some incomprehensible love song. And, inevitably, at the end of one of these numbers there is the clicked-on burst of recorded applause, which somehow manages to sound like a tap running full blast into a half-filled bath tub.

With the possible exception of Nazism, I can think of nothing in this wide world I detest as much as canned applause. No, that's wrong. There's one thing worse: canned laughter. It is natural that there should be some indication of audience reaction at the end of a song, dance or comedy routine. Psychologically, it gives the viewer a sense of participation, a feeling that he is part of an audience that is responding to a performance. To eliminate audience reaction is wrong, I believe, because it deprives the viewer of that sense of involvement. But canned applause is not the answer.

It has always been my contention that a studio audience for a variety show is an absolute essential—it is, indeed, a vital element of the show itself, not merely a luxury to be added where or when it is convenient.

The CBC has not always agreed with me. As far back as my early discussions with CBC officials about The Barris Beat, I can remember this difference of opinion. I don't mean that the CBC was or is against having a studio audience, but merely that it isn't regarded as very important. I think it is.

The fact is that in Toronto we simply do not have any theatre-studio in which an audience can be properly accommodated. We should have; we should have had at least one long ago; but we still don't. So, we make do with studios that were never intended to hold audiences. This means they are usually seated on wooden benches (as in the Pierce-Arrow Showroom) and that they can neither see nor hear very well. Most of the equipment—cameras, microphone booms, et cetera—is between the audience and the performers. It creates enough of a distraction so that the audience cannot really pay attention to what's going on in front of the cameras—which is really what they are there to see and take part in by reacting to it.

In order for a studio audience to serve its function—that is, to laugh or applaud and, more important, to be heard on the home sets laughing or applauding—there must be loudspeakers so they can hear what is said and microphones to pick up their reactions. In a studio not built to hold an audience, this is very difficult and most technicians would rather turn down the volume of the audience loudspeakers and microphones than risk getting "feedback" on the broadcast microphones. When that happens, the technicians are reported (or "logged") and presumably reprimanded. Therefore, they find it preferable to play it safe and keep the volume down. That this practice helps destroy the contribution of the studio audience to the success of a show fails to move the technicians. Playing it safe is contagious.

Over the years, I have argued this point tirelessly, and only occasionally won it. Whenever I have tried to have a camera moved so it will not block the vision of the studio audience I have been reminded that "we are doing shows not for a hundred or two hundred people in a studio audience but for the millions at home."

Of course, I recognize that point. But the success of certain types of variety shows (from Ed Sullivan to Johnny Carson) depends partly on the studio audience—and the proper use of it. If you do a comedy blackout, for example, and the studio audience misses the punchline—spoken or visual—because they cannot see or hear properly, the producer or his superior will react negatively: that wasn't very funny, because the studio audience didn't laugh, so we'd better not risk any further attempts at comedy. And since the home audience is conditioned by the studio audience, the effect of an inert studio audience can be to harm a show in the eyes of the millions. Thus, by creating (or settling for) conditions whereby a studio audience is rendered relatively useless, the network contributes to undermining the success of a show, and then complains that the show "isn't working."

I am not, incidentally, entirely alone in this view. As long ago as 1957, Stuart Griffiths, who was then one of the more forward-looking CBC officials, and Norman Jewison tried to persuade the Corporation to buy or lease a Toronto movie house that was up for grabs. It could fairly easily have been converted into a rather good theatre-studio, specifically for shows that require studio audiences. But there was no money; or, at least, what money there was had to be spent on more "urgent" needs.

I can remember attending a press conference, at about the same time, held by Alphonse Ouimet, then the head of the CBC. After outlining some of the plans the Corporation had in mind for the future, he threw the conference open to questions. I asked if the CBC had any plans for building or acquiring a theatre-studio that could accommodate audiences. I might as well have been a disgruntled actor complaining about the need for an extra mirror in a dressing room. Mr. Ouimet dismissed the question with some vague remark about the CBC trying to meet all reasonable requirements in due time.

It's easy enough to conclude that one could hardly expect Mr. Ouimet to concern himself with such matters, or even to understand their relevance. He was, after all, essentially an administrator who had many other problems to cope with. What was—and is—disturbing is the failure of others in the CBC (department heads, supervisors, even some producers) to recognize the importance of such a matter.

Only a few years ago, in 1966, a producer with whom I was working became enthusiastic about acquiring a small theatre in Toronto for TV shows. The theatre was, as it happened, available for lease and the money involved would not have been so great—about three hundred dollars a week per show if three shows a week were done there, which was plausible enough. Everyone in the CBC to whom he spoke agreed it was a good idea—but nobody could see a way of doing it. The money simply was not available for such an expenditure. This, in the same year that the CBC opened its twelve-million-dollar International Broadcasting Centre at Expo—a magnificent edifice with the latest in electronic equipment, broadloomed corridors, posh executive lounge—everything but a theatre-studio.

These days there is much talk about the new CBC television centre with which Toronto is to be favored. At this writing, I have not yet seen nor heard about any of the details of this centre, although I imagine the plans are well under way. But past experience leads me to believe there will be more "urgent" needs than a theatre-studio. Past experience leads me to believe the new centre will have the most expensive, most sophisticated equipment—everything possible to achieve technical perfection in future TV programs. Past experience leads me to believe that the producers, directors, technical producers, lighting directors, cameramen and other technical personnel will master all this fine new equipment and play their games with great skill. And past experience leads me to believe that all these resources, all this equipment, all this technical skill will not result in the creation of one Canadian television star.

But what does it matter, after all? The producer will go on playing his electronic games, prerecording everything, dazzling himself and his colleagues with his wizardry, pretending he has "reached" the audience by cueing the sound effects man to push the button that releases the burst of canned applause at the end of each eye-filling prerecorded production. And the bewildered performer will probably give up, move to the United States, slug it out for a few years, perhaps become established as something of a "name," and be invited back here (at a much higher fee than any resident performer can get) to appear in a special in which he will be billed proudly as "Canada's own."

And Now a Word From—

There's an old show business saw about everybody having two businesses—his own and show business. What this really means is that everyone in show business resents the fact that people outside the business feel qualified and entitled to function as critics. This presumption on the part of the public is not exactly indefensible. The logic is clear enough: "It's my money. I have a right to decide for myself whether it's a good show or a lousy one."

I suppose it's equally understandable that the person in show business—at whatever level—feels somewhat differently. The outsider, the "civilian," has no notion of what problems a show may face, no insight into the reasons something is done one way and not another, no understanding of the possibilities or the limitations of a particular show. The producer or writer or star may work like a slave to achieve a desired effect, only to have the public dismiss the whole thing with a snide remark or, worse still, a yawn. But of course that's the nature of the business and nothing will change it. Just as the customer doesn't care *why* his new car is imperfect, he doesn't concern himself with why a show isn't to his liking. The customer—the public—may not always be right, but he has the right to be wrong.

In fact, most show business people have a kind of foggy reverence for the public and are, perhaps remarkably, more receptive to the public's judgment than to that of the professional critic. The words of a critic can sting an actor; the public's apathy will be accepted philosophically. You will hear far more actors dismiss, with false bravado, the view of a critic ("What the hell does he know?") than the absence of an audience.

One reason for this is that the public is often easier to please than the critic. The professional critic tends to become jaded. He sees so many shows and finds so many of them similar that he wearies of the process after a while and can't bring himself to become enthused over the latest entry. Then, too, critics tend to have higher standards than the public—or they like to think they do, anyway.

The average man puts down his money for a theatre or movie ticket and is more or less content to be diverted for a couple of hours. The critic wants to be stimulated, surprised. He expects the theatre to aim higher than just diversion; he wants film to "say something" or explore new directions; he wants each new book to be outstanding; he expects television to aim for a higher level than it usually does.[1]

I don't want, at this point, to go into the whole field of television criticism. It's a subject that deserves—and will receive—separate attention later.

But there is another kind of critic, a very special kind, who merits discussion here. He is important because, like the professional critic writing in a newspaper or magazine, he wields a good deal of influence. He really has more pull than the man paid as a professional critic. This is the sponsor— the man who pays the piper in television and feels entitled to call the tune. Make no mistake about it—he does feel so entitled. Whether he should be allowed to is another matter. What is important is that he does.

The sponsor is a man with money who is asked to spend it to pay for a television program or series. When he agrees to do so, he does it for one reason and one reason alone— to advertise and thereby sell his product. Not to employ Canadian talent, not to entertain the Canadian public, not to uplift the cultural taste of the country, certainly not to create a healthy climate for the arts and prevent artists from going elsewhere. Such lofty matters are for the consideration of network and union officials, Royal Commissions, and Saturday supplement think-piece writers. The sponsor uses

---

[1] The "civilian" often resents the critic for a different reason: the critic makes him feel insecure. The theatre-goer attends the opening of a frothy new musical, finds it reasonably enjoyable, then picks up the next day's paper only to read that the show was banal, thin, artificial, inept, et cetera. This strikes at his own taste and judgment, so he resents the highbrow critic.

The painted backdrop of the Toronto skyline was really too good to be wasted on a minor show, but I was glad to have it.

With Eva Gabor at a fund-raising appearance. At left is Ben Nobleman, then Toronto B'nai B'rith publicist.

Working with Bing Crosby on an Easter Seal show for CFTO was a rare treat. Crosby was truly a gentleman as well as a hard-working professional.

"Bonanza" star Lorne Greene starred in the CNE Grandstand show the year I wrote it. His act, a smash hit in Las Vegas, was yawned at by Toronto critics.

Above, two shots taken during the brief run of "Barris & Company." Below left, with Tessie O'Shea, and right with Celia Franca and Yves Montand.

television exactly as he uses newspaper or magazine ads, or billboards or circular letters. The main difference is that he usually spends a lot more money on television than he ever did in other advertising media. The main similarity is that, like newspapers, television vitally needs the advertiser's money in order to exist.

This man, this sponsor, is not an ogre. He is a human being with human strengths and weaknesses and needs. He is a successful businessman with a brain and skills and emotions. When his tooth hurts he goes to his dentist. When he needs an operation he goes to a surgeon. When his car is sick he takes it to the car hospital. Just like everybody else. When he wants the most effective way to advertise his product for sale he goes to an advertising agency, whose business it is to guide and advise its clients on just such matters. The ad agency is equipped and qualified to advise the sponsor. The man who runs the agency is an expert in his field—that's why the sponsor goes to him, as he would to a dentist, a doctor or a mechanic. Now, I doubt very much if the average sponsor tells his dentist how to drill a tooth, or his surgeon how to remove an appendix, or his mechanic how to do whatever it is that mechanics do under the hoods of cars. These men are experts and their value is respected and recognized. "Fix it," each customer orders, and when it is fixed he pays the bill.

But for some reason the sponsor (the same man) is incapable of treating the ad agency as an "expert"—even though that's the whole idea of going to an agency in the first place. He is even less capable of allowing the same recognition to the network executive, or the producer, or a writer or performer on a show. By the very act of accepting his money for their services they have apparently lost the respect which he demonstrated in them by going to them— as if they were all prostitutes of whom he expected virginity.

The sponsor feels very close to his money—especially when such large amounts of it are involved—and is reluctant to part with it without exercising some judgment over how it is spent. Quite naturally, he has the power of the final decision over which particular program or series he will sponsor. But very often that isn't enough—he likes to get right down there in the nitty-gritty and fool around with *how* the program is put together, who's on it and what's to be said or done on it. And if he and the "experts" disagree, guess who gets his way.

When Norman Jewison went to New York to work as a television director, one of his early assignments was to direct a series called "The Big Party," to be sponsored by the Revlon company, manufacturers of cosmetics. Jewison later recalled his first meeting with Charles Revson, head of the Revlon firm. This hard-headed businessman began advising Jewison on how to do the program. Not how to make lipstick, or even how to sell lipstick—but how to direct a live TV variety show. Jewison smiled uneasily and said, "Surely, Mr. Revson, you don't intend to get involved in the actual production of this series, do you?" "You're damn right I do," snapped the sponsor. "If I didn't intend to get involved, I would have bought a goddam filmed program."

Not alone because of Revson's "involvement," Jewison quit the show after a few weeks. The program itself expired in midseason. It deserved to. It wasn't a good show. And one of the reasons was the insistence by the sponsor that he knew better how to put on a successful TV program than did the very people he had hired to do it. But of course nobody will ever convince Mr. Revson of that. Sponsors will pour millions of dollars into television programs. If a program advised by an agency or a network doesn't succeed—and by that is meant increasing the sale of his product, not merely entertaining the audience—the sponsor will abandon the program and, very often, move his lucrative account to a different ad agency.

I suppose it's inevitable, therefore, that agencies tend to be very cautious in recommending TV programs to their clients and also in approving the content of each program. The ad agency is paid a fee of from seventeen to twenty per cent of whatever the sponsor spends on a program. The agency is loathe to lose this considerable fee by allowing a program to displease a sponsor. The same applies to the networks. In U.S. television, the power of the sponsor is not necessarily greater—it is simply acknowledged more openly. The CBC likes to pretend it is not subject to the whims of sponsors, that it makes its own decisions. But this is only partly true; it's a matter of degree.

Perhaps the point can be demonstrated this way. A network comes up with a program proposal and presents it to the agencies. One agency likes the show and recommends it to a particular client. If the client (the potential sponsor) doesn't like the idea, he'll decline to buy it. This decreases the chances of the program's getting on the air.[1]

But let us say the sponsor likes the program idea generally but doesn't like the mustache worn by a particular performer or actor. In the United States, the man with the offending brush will be advised to shave it off or he'll be replaced. In Canada, an attempt will be made to persuade him that he really looks better without the mustache; no reference will be made to the fact that the suggestion originated with the sponsor. But either way, the sponsor's wishes are acted on.

It isn't always quite that simple or straightforward, of course. One of the problems is that sometimes network or agency people will try to anticipate the likes and dislikes of a sponsor—to avoid trouble before it arises, to cross a bridge before they come to it. Sometimes the sponsors are blameless. Ad agency executives or network officials will make decisions concerning some supposedly delicate area that might not really be so delicate. It just seems safer that way.

A CBC spokesman will sometimes boast that the sponsor has little or no say in programming, that decisions are made by the Corporation. But often it is an empty boast, because the decisions are made with full awareness of the wishes of a sponsor—or, at least, in anticipation of those wishes. It's a little like a playwright in the U.S.S.R. boasting that his works are never censored; they are not censored because he is smart enough to know in advance what will be allowed and what will not be. And rather than risk the wrath of the censor (or sponsor) he will avoid those tricky areas. Whatever the truth of such claims, I have known instances where sponsors (or their agencies) took a stubborn stand and others where they were reasonable.

On a program I did last year, a scheduled guest was Nancy

---

[1] At the CBC, certain kinds of programs, such as news and public affairs, are never offered for sponsorship, so they live or die at the discretion of the network brass.

Greene. One of our sponsors was Chrysler; Miss Greene was already doing commercials for General Motors. The Chrysler people agreed to her appearance on our show. The GM agency also agreed, but was later overruled by their client—General Motors didn't want Nancy on a Chrysler show. (Notice, by the way, that the CBC, whose program it was, had no say in the whole matter.)

After Flashback had been on the air for some time, a change of sponsors was coming about. Chrysler was to be one of the new sponsors. Bill Walker, then host of the show, was "identified" with Ford, having done many commercials for that company. The CBC told Walker he'd either have to drop any future Ford commercials or withdraw from the show. He withdrew and was replaced by Jimmy Tapp. Incidentally, Walker later claimed that he had learned the Ford company would have been happy to pick up sponsorship of Flashback—thus eliminating the "sponsor conflict" issue— but the CBC never offered the program to Ford.

There have also been incidents where the CBC has proven stubborn, sometimes to its own detriment. Some years back a program called "Graphic" was created. It was a magazine-type public affairs show with Joe McCulley as host. Ford agreed to buy it for a trial thirteen-week period but felt the program should be known as "Ford Graphic." The CBC said no, it was a matter of policy not to use the name of a sponsor in the title of a show. The Ford agency pointed out that the same CBC was then presenting a series on the air called "General Motors Presents." But the CBC said that was "different." Ford gave in and agreed to sponsor the program for the first thirteen weeks, without its name in the title. Just as option time was approaching (along about the ninth or tenth week) an incident occurred that demonstrated how "brave" the CBC can be in dealing with sponsors.

National Safe Driving Week was approaching and the agency requested that in closing the show, McCulley should urge his viewers to drive safely. The program's supervising producer objected, maintaining that this was an additional commercial message, over and above the number of commercials allowed. The admonition to drive safely was ruled out.

The next day, sensing somebody had goofed, the CBC

called Ford's agency placatingly and said it had been decided that after the first thirteen weeks, Ford would be allowed to have its name in the title of the show—"Ford Graphic" would be the new name.

But it was too late. The previous night's foolish incident had so angered the sponsors that Ford cancelled its sponsorship of the show, instead of renewing.

One thing a sponsor dislikes above all—and the agencies and networks know it—is any mention of a rival product on his program. (Networks, incidentally, are often just as queasy about the mention of a rival network.) It matters not what is said about the rival product—the mere mention of it in a script strikes fear into the heart of an agency representative or a network official.

Many years ago there was a CBC program called "Pick the Star," on which new talent was given a chance to perform and compete for awards. On the first program in the series, the host, the late Dick MacDougall, introduced the first contestant and chatted with the young man for a few minutes before asking him to sing. At the conclusion of this talk, MacDougall wished the contestant good luck. It was the last time he was permitted to indulge in this particular courtesy. The sponsor of the program was a manufacturer of margarine—and "Good Luck" was the name of a rival brand of margarine.

On another early CBC television series, "Holiday Ranch," a highly successful guest performer was comedienne Libby Morris. However, after her first appearance she was banned from the show. Reason: the sponsor was Aylmer and, as any Canadian housewife knows, Aylmer and Libby are rival brands of canned foods.

These are not isolated examples, "exceptions" that prove the rule. They are commonplace. There was a famous incident in U.S. television, when a highly regarded drama series planned a program dealing with the atrocities in Nazi Germany. The sponsor (or, quite possibly, the agency) felt uneasy about the delicacy of the matter and refused to be associated with this particular drama. Reason: the sponsor was a gas company and the association with Hitler's infamous gas ovens was one the company didn't especially consider helpful to its "image."

The subject of cigaret smoking and its relationship to lung cancer has caused more than one TV network to tread softly. Cigaret manufacturers formed a quick aversion to hospital scenes or anything that might suggest ill health. Once, when I was writing the Juliette Show, we planned a short music-and-comedy sketch that was a take-off on the "Medic" series, then quite popular on TV. It was innocous enough, hardly dealing with health or medicine, but showing Julie as a nurse and George Murray as a doctor. Nevertheless, the sketch was cancelled. The sponsors, Player's Cigarets, didn't think any sort of hospital scene was in good taste. Or, at least, that's what the producer said the agency said the sponsor had said.

And it was no coincidence that the headline-making stories about the development of the Strickman filter were ignored by Front Page Challenge for a couple of years. When the story first broke, the program was sponsored by Du Maurier Cigarets and although nobody ever said in so many words that the sponsor didn't want us to do the story, everyone concerned was aware that it was a "delicate" area. There was nothing delicate about the story itself—only in the face of the identity of the sponsor. Eventually, the story was done—after Du Maurier had dropped the show and a new (non-cigaret) sponsor was paying for the program.

I was once associated with a program sponsored by Chrysler. At one writers' meeting, somebody came up with an Edsel joke. (Edsel jokes are standard because that short-lived automobile model invites ridicule.) Even though the joke would have been a knock at an extinct automobile, we decided not to do it—for fear that the Chrysler people would not appreciate even a mention of a rival company's product. And, heaven help me, I was among those who favored this decision.

Sponsor sensitivity—or agency and network sensitivity to possible sponsor sensitivity—is not restricted to variety shows. Years ago, when the CBC was producing a series called "General Motors Presents," the agency, on behalf of the sponsor, as always, shot down so many proposed drama scripts that those involved with the series nicknamed it "General Motors Prevents."

I think my very favorite story concerning sponsor (or agency) interference with a program is one that happened some years ago on a program called "Here's Duffy." This was the year following The Barris Beat's run and I was a guest of Jack Duffy's one week. The writers, Peppiatt, Aylesworth and Manings, as I recall, had come up with a series of vignettes about different kinds of annoying people one runs into while travelling. In these, Duffy played the victimized character, and I was the nuisance.

In one of them, Duffy was supposed to encounter me at an airport terminal. He would ask me to mind his luggage while he went to get a cup of coffee. "Coffee?" I was to respond, horrified. "Coffee is poison when you're travelling. Here, I've got some pills that will be good for you." And so on.

That was the way we rehearsed it on show day. Well, it so happened that the program was sponsored by Salada Tea and that some visiting brass from the agency were on hand during the rehearsal. After the dress rehearsal, one of the ad agency men took aside Bill Davis, the producer, and told him he didn't think it was such a hot idea to mention coffee on a program sponsored by a tea company. Too busy to argue, Davis passed the word along to Duffy, suggesting the reference be changed to tea. Unfortunately, nobody told me.

When we got to that point in the show (and, remember, this was now on the air, live) Duffy came up to me, dropped his luggage and asked me to mind it while he went to have a cup of tea. I had no choice but to go along with the change. "Tea?" I shouted. "Tea is poison when you're flying!" Only then did the smart boys in the client's booth realize what they had wrought.

At the CBC, it has always been a matter of rigid policy to neither solicit nor accept advertising on news and public affairs programs. The theory, voiced many times by the CBC, is that not only should news not be sponsored but it should not even "appear" to be sponsored—presumably because a sponsor might try to suppress news stories unfavorable to him in some way. I seriously doubt that the theory holds water.

Whatever faults the news programs on U.S. television may have, I am not aware that Huntley and Brinkley or Walter Cronkite are any less reliable or candid because their networks sell advertising time for deodorants, tooth pastes, canned soups or cosmetics on their newscasts.

To take a couple of glaring examples, automobile manufacturers and cigaret makers are among the biggest-spending television sponsors on this continent. I don't think it can be demonstrated that the CBC reported any more fully than did the American networks the Ralph Nader attacks on automobile safety, or the various medical reports warning smokers of the danger of cancer. The CBC's no-sponsorship policy on news also means that the network deprives itself of considerable revenue. Our other Canadian network, CTV, allows sponsorship of such programs. It might well be argued that CTV is able to cover and present news more fully and more attractively because of the increased revenue at its disposal—revenue which the CBC desperately needs but coldly declines.

Nevertheless, the CBC is adamant on this point. One need only recall the Earl Cameron incident. Cameron, a staff announcer who delivered the CBC National News for years, earned extra income by doing commercials for Crest Toothpaste and American Motors. Some CBC affiliate stations could not resist the temptation to place some of these commercials immediately preceding or immediately following the newscasts—thus running afoul of the CBC dictum that news broadcasts shall neither be sponsored nor "appear to be" sponsored. In fact, the use of these commercials at such times in no way affected the content or viewpoint of the CBC news.

Since the CBC apparently has no jurisdiction over what commercials an affiliate station may use, or how, the scapegoat had to be Earl Cameron. He was given his choice of either giving up the extra income from the commercials or being reassigned to another CBC duty. He chose the latter course, but in effect he lost both ways—because his greatest value to any sponsors was his exposure on the coast-to-coast late night news. When he was removed from that spot (and given the less prestigious and less widely viewed early evening newscast) the sponsors soon lost interest in him.

The CBC also tends to be excessively pussyfooted about "plugs." A plug is, in effect, an unpaid-for mention of a product or service. It is understandable that a network (like a newspaper) should be reluctant to give away what it is in business to sell. What is less realistic is the Corporation's unwillingness to accept a service or an act of co-operation which it often needs—because it does not like to acknowledge such a service with a plug.

In American television (and to some extent on CTV) airlines and hotels frequently get credit for extending "courtesies" to visiting performers. That simply means that a guest for a program will be flown free to New York from Hollywood, or vice versa, in exchange for a brief mention of this fact at the end of the show. Or that a certain hotel will agree to accommodate the cast of a show without charge for this same mention. Very often—and particularly in Canadian television—just such an expense item can make the difference between being able to afford a certain guest or even a certain show and not being able to. But the CBC steadfastly refuses to allow such plugs.

It goes further than that. I have been associated with programs where the budget will not allow for clothes to be made at the CBC's expense for a performer. A clothier will be more than willing to supply the wardrobe in exchange for acknowledgment of this service—at the end of a program, one more item in the long list of credits that roll by the viewer's eye. The CBC almost invariably refuses such an arrangement.

When a visiting author mentions his book or holds up a copy of it on, say, Front Page Challenge, the producer of the program will usually receive a terse memo from something called the Sales Acceptance Department of the CBC, reminding him that the Corporation is against such plugs. This is the worst form of hypocrisy. Everyone knows the author is there to talk about his book, in hopes of stimulating its sale. More often than not, he agrees to appear on the program for a nominal fee simply to plug his book. The program is happy to have him because he is celebrated, or fascinating or controversial. But the CBC still frowns disapprovingly when he plugs his book.

In such inane ways does the CBC cling, rather pathetically, to the romantic notion that it is above the market place, that it cannot be intimidated or influenced by sponsors or anyone who might conceivably become a sponsor, and that its airwaves cannot be penetrated by greedy commercially-minded publicity hounds. And yet, such unseemly protestations of virtue—somewhat like a pregnant woman claiming virginity—can't be taken too seriously by anyone who has worked around the CBC for a few years.

There was a time when the CBC planned and executed its programs without regard for the wishes or tastes of potential sponsors. When the program was all nicely put together, the CBC went to the agencies and said: "Here it is, take it or leave it." Fortunately or not—depending on your viewpoint—this is simply no longer true. It began to change and the whole CBC began to change (the Pierce-Arrow Showroom began leaking) at about the time the Liberals were defeated in 1957 and the Progressive Conservatives came to power, committed to strip away some of the CBC's powers.

Gradually the CBC has been forced to recognize the role of the sponsor, at least in certain areas of programming—notably variety and drama. It still clings to the unbusinesslike notion that plugs are unseemly. But it can no longer claim that it is never influenced by the likes or dislikes of sponsors. Occasionally, it still indulges in that luxury, but not as stubbornly as it once did.

You may regard this as a kind of progress. I am not sure I do. I know that those pre-1958 days were the Golden Age of television variety in Canada. I know that the Corporation offered far more programming, much of it better than will be found today; developed far more talent; employed far more performers, actors, writers, directors and musicians than it does now.

It is true that it also displeased more sponsors (possibly also more viewers, although that's debatable) than it does now. But those sponsors survived. They are still around, and they are sponsoring more American programs on Canadian television than they did in those days. They almost have to—there aren't that many Canadian programs being offered to them any more.

The Saturday Night Problem

I think it's only human nature that anyone who fails to achieve his goal on the first try wants a second chance. The ball player itches for another turn at bat, the gambler wants another roll on the dice, the scientist goes back to his lab, the novelist rewrites, the film director does retakes, the lawyer appeals a decision, the doctor operates again.

Call it vanity, or whatever, but I confess that after the old Barris Beat program went off the air, back in 1958, I hoped for a while that it might be revived, in some form. As the years passed, however, and I became absorbed in all kinds of other work, such thoughts eventually went out of my mind.

True, in 1960, when CFTO-TV was about to begin broadcasting, I tried to land a late-night spot on that station, to do a talk-cum-variety program. But, as related earlier, Rick Campbell won that spot. A few years after that, there was some loose talk around the CBC of a new show with me. At the time, I had an agent (a funny lady who later turned theatrical producer and then skipped the country rather than cope with a stack of debts) who told me the CBC was "considering" some sort of revival of The Barris Beat. But this turned out to be just talk.

In December, 1966, when A World of Music had just been cancelled, I had a talk with Ken Gunton, who was my second writer on that show. Gunton was an old friend. He had been the first studio director I'd ever worked with, on the old Eleven Thirty Friday shows and in the early weeks of The Barris Beat. He had left the CBC, worked at an ad agency and later as a director of TV commercials. He had only recently developed an interest in television writing and A World of Music had been his first regular assignment.

Ken and I began wondering aloud whether some sort of late night talk-plus-variety program wouldn't be a good candidate for the Saturday night post-hockey spot. The CBC had already decided on a show called "In Person" to finish out that season in place of A World Of Music. But we were thinking beyond that—the 1967/68 season.

We had a series of meetings to discuss the idea and soon came up with a detailed presentation in writing, which I took to Len Starmer, the superintendent of light entertainment. He read it, said there was some merit in the idea, but added he could take no action on it at the time.

The following spring, I discussed the matter again with Starmer and we agreed that I might be host of one of the In Person shows (they were using various hosts that season) and do the program more or less along the lines I preferred, so that this particular edition of In Person might serve as a kind of unofficial pilot for future reference. Working with producer Mark Warren, I did the show that May, using Johnny Wayne, Betty Robertson, Aubrey Tadman and Peter Appleyard as guests. It went reasonably well, but that was that. No more was heard of the matter.

In Person completed its season and was renewed for another, but with Al Hamel signed as permanent host. Like A World Of Music before it, In Person never achieved anything like the ratings the Juliette Show had once had—the CBC still had not solved "the Saturday night problem."

And so, in December of 1967 (a year after the original suggestion) I again brought up the subject of a talk-and-variety show for that time slot, with me as "host." This time, I detected a glimmer of encouragement in Starmer's reaction. He indicated that the Corporation might go for the idea, but he wasn't certain I was the right man for the job. He wondered aloud what my reaction would be if they decided to do the program, but with somebody else as host.

I said that if that happened I'd be sorry, but that I couldn't do very much about it. I could hardly lay claim to having invented such a format. My argument was that there should be such a show on Canadian television—to give exposure in an informal atmosphere to Canadian (and visiting) personalities, just as the Carson, Allen, Bishop, Griffin and Douglas shows were doing in the United States for American personalities. I felt it was a show I could do, it was one I wanted to do. But if the CBC decided on someone else, I couldn't stop them.

During the winter, I had several talks with Starmer and also with Bruce Raymond, then the director of the English language network. They kept saying they were "interested" in the idea, but would not commit themselves. In our presentation to Starmer, Gunton and I had recommended that this proposed program be done "live." But this posed a problem: how to cope with a live show immediately following the hockey game, when the length of the games was always uncertain.

This hockey business is rather complex and I had better take time to try explaining it now. On most Saturday nights between October and May, there are two NHL games played in Canada—one in Toronto, one in Montreal. The CBC's policy has long been to alternate between them in feeding a game to the full CBC network. On one Saturday, the Toronto game goes on the "major" network and the Montreal game is seen on a "minor" network, in and around Montreal. The following week, Canadians across the country see the Montreal game, except for the Toronto area, where the Toronto game is seen.

Up to this time, the show following hockey was on video-tape, whether it was Juliette (except in the early days before video-tape existed) or A World of Music or In Person. These shows always ran thirty minutes, which meant that they could not be expected to end at exactly 11 P.M. (Eastern Standard Time), when the CBC's National News went on the air. The games might end anywhere between 10:15 and 10:30, or possibly later. And, of course, it was extremely unlikely both games would ever end at exactly the same time.

The system used until then was that if one game ended early, the wrap-up period (summing up of highlights, giving the league standings, etc.) would be "stretched" until the second game ended. Thus, the network could then be "joined" and the thirty-minute post-hockey show would be telecast.

This would run to anywhere between 10:45 to 10:58 and the slack would be taken up, until 11 P.M., with an unpretentious sports program on which Jim Coleman would interview some sports figure for two, three or ten minutes. Then, the National News would go on.

However—and this gets still more complicated—any sponsor buying the post-hockey half hour had to be assured of a thirty-minute show and if either of the hockey games ran later than 10:30, then the news would have to be delayed by a few minutes, whatever amount of time was needed to finish the half-hour video-taped show that had started after the completion of *both* hockey games. This did occur occasionally, I found out, and nobody seemed to mind. The news might be a few minutes late starting, but nobody bothered checking his watch, or if they did they were content to wait a few minutes for the news.

In our presentation, we had suggested our show be done live—partly because of the freshness thus offered, but mainly to eliminate this gap between the end of the show and the National News—a gap during which many viewers would be likely to switch to another channel. We wanted our show to run from the end of the game right up to 11 P.M., with no gap. Everyone agreed this was a desirable—if tricky—goal.

And so, on into March our periodic talks dragged, with Starmer always indicating that the chances looked good, but still unable to make a commitment. During these talks, another subject came up. It would be worthwhile if the show could resume after the news and run until midnight, thus giving us a longer period. One of the glaring flaws in our presentation was the short length of time allowed for a program of this type.

All the similar U.S. programs ran from sixty to ninety minutes, and nightly, at that. All we'd have would be thirty to forty minutes once a week. So the idea of extending the length by resuming the program at about 11:15, after the news, was appealing. But Starmer made it clear he had little hope of achieving this on our first season. If the show worked out (if, indeed, it ever got on) this would be a goal to aim for the following season.

Sometime in April, Len Starmer told me the network

had now definitely sanctioned the idea of the program. He added, with what I considered singularly unflattering candor, that they had thought and thought but simply could not come up with anyone they felt was better qualified than I to do the show. The next logical subject was to decide on a producer and a director for the program. Starmer felt, and I agreed, that we should split the jobs—one man producing, another directing.

A few days later, Starmer told me he had discussed the program idea with Stan Jacobson, a producer-director of some experience and some good credits, and found Jacobson very interested in doing it. He did say that Stan had expressed some doubts as to whether I was the best man for the show, but he was willing to try. All this came as a bit of a surprise to me, because Jacobson had been talking of moving to Hollywood. But Starmer said the idea of this new show had "excited" Jacobson enough so that he wanted to do it.

(My years at the CBC, I'm afraid, have taught me to be a little bit suspicious. It is usually when someone is talking of leaving that he becomes suddenly highly regarded. There is little doubt in my mind that Starmer dangled this new show in front of Jacobson in an effort to dissuade him from leaving for Hollywood.)

Nevertheless, I agreed to meet with Stan to discuss the show. The only request I made in advance was that Ken Gunton be signed as one of the writers (I, too, would be involved in the writing), since Ken and I had worked together in preparing and presenting the idea to the CBC and also because I felt Ken knew me well enough to have a grasp of what the program should be about. Starmer readily agreed to this.

My first meeting with Stan did not go well. I respect Jacobson and recognize his ability; further, I admire his candor. But we were clearly at odds in our understanding of what sort of show this was to be. When I talked of having such guests as Barbara Hamilton or Paul Kligman on the show, his reaction was: "What for?" He felt nobody would be interested in them. He said he was always "bored" when Johnny Carson introduced show business celebrities on his program and conversed with them. I felt differently;

I believed this had to be a basic part of the show we were to do.

I expressed my uneasiness to Starmer, but he told me not to worry, that Stan was "feeling his way," that there was no real conflict between our views, that I should give it time to work out.

Next, I learned that Stan wanted to do a pilot of the show. I was not wildly enthusiastic about this, mostly because I felt no pilot could truly represent the conditions under which we'd be doing a live show. But Starmer assured me it was worth doing if only as an exercise, a way of testing things. And, in any case, the pilot would never be aired.

Jacobson had signed a platoon of writers for the pilot: Gary Ferrier and Aubrey Tadman as head writers, plus a young team, Lorne Michaels and Hart Pomerantz; also Bill Lynn, one of the writers for the Tommy Hunter Show, and Ken Gunton and myself. I had nothing against any of these writers—although except for Gunton, the only one I knew was Tadman—but I was a little disturbed that Jacobson should hire them and also decree who would be the head writers without even so much as discussing the matter with me.

Starmer also began talking of a "permanent company" of revue performers or sketch players. I couldn't see the point of this, but he told me it was something that would be an asset to the show.

Gradually, it dawned on me that what Jacobson really was planning was a kind of Canadian version of Rowan and Martin's Laugh-In, with me simply there to "set up" the gags, sketches and blackouts. I expressed this view to both Starmer and Jacobson, but they assured me I was wrong.

After several frustrating meetings, I was convinced that Stan and I were talking about two different programs. I proposed that both of us go to Starmer and have it out. He agreed.

That meeting was a lively one, with both Stan and myself expressing our ideas about what the show should be—and proving simply that we were miles apart. Starmer again played the role of peace-maker, hoping to minimize our differences and resolve them. Stan said quite candidly that he

Riding a circus elephant is about as high as I ever want to get. Below, with old friend Norman Jewison, taken on a Hollywood set.

Writing two O'Keefe Centre specials gave me a chance to work with Rich Little and Al Hirt, above, and with Sandra O'Neill and George Burns.

didn't want to do a show he didn't believe in. I felt the same way and said so. If this show should fail, I wanted it to fail because *my* way was wrong, not because I had followed the tastes and wishes of somebody else who was wrong. Starmer tended to side with me, arguing that Canadian personalities should be on the show, that talk should be a basic part of it, et cetera. Jacobson said he could not agree.

After Jacobson left, I stayed behind to talk further with Starmer. He now said he realized Stan and I could not work together and he would simply have to assign another producer to the show. I felt relieved. But the very next day Starmer reversed himself. He told me he had decided to go along with Stan and that if I wanted to do the show, I'd have to revise my thinking to meet at least some of Stan's wishes.

That, I suppose, was when I should have packed it in and said no. But I went instead on the foot-in-the-door theory—first get the show, then fight the individual battles. So I agreed to try again to work things out with Stan.

By now, the title of the show had been decided on. At first, in accordance with the long-standing CBC tradition, Starmer was against the use of my name in the title of the show. In this instance, Jacobson disagreed with him.

I thought of the title "Barris & Company," and this was ultimately accepted. I didn't realize then how easily the title itself could cause misunderstandings. To me, Barris and Company meant simply that the program would have Barris and "company"—that is, guests, people dropping in to chat or perform. But to Jacobson (and apparently others at the CBC) it meant a company of performers, appearing regularly.

In the weeks following, we had numerous meetings—Stan, the writers and I—most of which ended in discord. Stan more than once announced he was withdrawing from the show. I didn't urge him not to. He wanted sketches and blackouts on the program and a minimum of conversation; he wanted no singer to sing "unless there's a reason for it" —meaning he wanted only satirical or topical songs performed on the show. I kept saying this was Laugh-In, he kept saying it wasn't. And Starmer kept assuring me that everything would be all right.

Finally, somehow, we managed to compromise enough to map out the pilot. Our pilot was a camel—a camel being Fred Allen's definition of a horse put together by a committee. It pleased neither me nor Stan, nor the CBC. If it proved anything, it proved that compromise never really works.

On that pilot, we had Gordon Sinclair (at my insistence) as a talking guest. His segment turned out to be the best thing on the pilot. We also had Sandra O'Neill, who sang two numbers and talked with me, very briefly. We had a band number (with Guido Basso and his orchestra) and some sketches and blackouts, most of which didn't work too well. And we had an audience participation segment, which also didn't work.

The day after we viewed the pilot, we all met to discuss its value. I felt it proved only that the talk on the show worked better than the sketches.

I also made an issue of the studio setup. Once again, we had a studio audience whose vision was blocked by cameras and other equipment, thus dissipating their enjoyment of the program. I felt the set (designed by Bill Zaharuk along lines suggested by Jacobson) was all wrong. It was a kind of horseshoe-shaped set, with the band at one end, me at the other and the audience in the centre. I felt this was wrong because the shape tended to focus attention towards the centre—where the sketches were performed; but I was off at one end of it, so that I wasn't even facing the audience.

I suggested that sometime during the summer (the show was to begin in the fall) a group of us go to New York to watch the Johnny Carson operation, to see how their studio setup coped with the problems of cameras in the way of the audience, etc. Everyone agreed this was a splendid idea, but even though I pressed several times during the summer for this, nothing ever came of it.

Even before the pilot had been video-taped, Stan Jacobson had announced his intention of going to Hollywood for the summer. Whether or not he returned would depend on how well he did out there. This bothered me because I felt the summer months were vital for planning our programs, which could hardly be done with the producer two thousand miles from Toronto. But Stan had made his plans and couldn't very well change them.

The matter of a director still remained unresolved. For the pilot, Jacobson had both produced and directed, but we were still supposed to have a director named for the series. Stan had someone in mind, but no one could be appointed yet, with Stan's own status as producer still uncertain.

Stan went off to Hollywood in mid-June and Starmer said he was giving Stan until July 15 to decide whether or not he'd come back to do our show. Stan had said he intended to come back, at least long enough to "launch" the show, even if he was going to move permanently to Hollywood. But, of course, this could not be considered a definite commitment.

The decision came earlier than expected, and more at Starmer's instigation than Stan's. Well before July 15, Starmer told me that he had pressed Jacobson for a decision. Stan had felt he hadn't been in Hollywood long enough to assess fairly his future there. Since he needed more time and Starmer wanted an immediate decision, Stan was virtually forced to withdraw from our program. Starmer told me Bob Jarvis would be my producer. I was pleased at this news, not necessarily because I considered him a "better" producer than Jacobson, but because I had worked many times with him in the past and felt I had a better relationship with Jarvis. Also, since Stan and I had disagreed so markedly before and during the making of the pilot, I felt we'd start fresh with Jarvis and perhaps get back closer to the show I wanted to do—and which, indeed, the CBC had agreed to do.

My spirits rose, somewhat. We were going to start all over again, perhaps learning from the mistakes of the pilot.

The matter of a director had to be settled, and this dragged on for some weeks. Jarvis wanted to use Pat King, his studio director for some time and a young man in whom Jarvis believed. Starmer was against this—partly because he didn't share Bob's faith in King, partly because he had other directors available and couldn't justify promoting a studio director to director under the circumstances.

Starmer suggested Terry Kyne as our director, but Jarvis and I both balked. The reason was simple: Kyne had been producer-director of Nightcap, a very specialized sort of satirical program, and we didn't want to risk the possibility that he would try to shape this new program into an imitation or extension of Nightcap, which was now off the air. Kyne eventually solved the problem himself by deciding to leave the CBC. Thus Jarvis was able to get his original choice of Pat King approved by Starmer.

Jarvis had also cut down the writing staff somewhat, a move I approved of. Since we did not intend to do as much prepared comedy material as Jacobson had wanted, there was no need for six or seven writers. Lorne Michaels and Hart Pomerantz had already left for Hollywood to write the Phyllis Diller Show. Bill Lynn had withdrawn to take on another CBC project. This left Ferrier, Tadman, Gunton and myself. We felt it was enough.

On the pilot we had used Alex Trebek, an announcer, as a sort of sidekick for me. None of us had liked the results. Trebek seemed too snarky, too determined to assert himself, and somewhat negative about the whole show.

We decided to go in another direction—to use a girl. It would be better if she were an "unknown" and not a professional performer, we felt. She could be eased gradually into the show, contributing more if she worked out and was accepted by audiences, or eased out if she didn't and wasn't. Jarvis interviewed dozens of girls and narrowed them down to about ten, whom we then auditioned in a studio.

The girl we decided on was Janet Baird, a tall, blonde English girl who worked at an advertising agency and had a kind of independent air about her.

Almost from the first meeing we had with Pat King, I sensed trouble. He, like Jacobson, seemed to feel the talk on the program would be a waste of time. He was all in favor of more singing, more performing, a few pretty girls to dress things up. Jarvis had already booked (with my concurrence) the guests for the first show: novelist Arthur Hailey, film director Paul Almond and his wife, actress

Genevieve Bujold. King was convinced they would be dull and dreary. (One of our writers, I blush to add, didn't even know who Hailey was.)

One thing that bothered me was that almost everyone—Pat King, Tadman and Ferrier and even Jarvis—kept distinguishing between talk and "entertainment" on the program, as if they felt the talk would not be entertaining. I, of course, felt that the talk would be the foundation of the show—largely because it would (or should) be entertaining. And whenever I suggested that I wanted more than five or six minutes to talk with a guest, I got worried frowns from everyone.

Pat King's biggest drawback, however, was his lack of experience as a director. In retrospect I think it was reckless and unfair to burden him with a new, relatively large-scale, network program—and a "live" one, at that—rather than let him break in on some other program, perhaps an established one on which there wouldn't be as much pressure.

Perhaps he sensed my misgivings about him. I certainly sensed his misgivings about the show. In any case, Pat and I didn't seem able to communicate with each other very well.

He displayed a fault so typical of CBC producer-directors: an inability or unwillingness to consider the host of a program as much more than a hired hand. He constantly made decisions in the studio without consulting me—decisions that frequently affected me directly. He rarely bothered to tell me what he was doing or why. He would have his studio director relay instructions to me without bothering to explain why this or that had been decided.

Particularly on a live show, changes in the running order or content of a show affect most the person on camera—and even more so in the kind of program we were doing, where I was supposedly the focal point of the show. Changes made without my knowledge inevitably resulted in my floundering around (on the air) without knowing what was to come next.

On the show, I usually came out, talked for a minute or so and then called for Janet to bring me a newspaper, from which I then picked items to comment on. One week, on the dress rehearsal, I called for Janet only to learn that she had been instructed to go to Guido Basso and the orchestra. The cameras would then take a shot of Janet and Guido and the whole orchestra—all reading newspapers. It was a cute idea, but nobody had bothered to tell me about it. Pat apologized later, saying he "forgot."

Another time, I was informed of a change—cutting out my monologue—only twenty seconds before air time. This meant I was to enter and immediately introduce the first guest, as it happened, the newly crowned Miss Canada. But the show had no sooner started than I was given frantic hand signals (while I was already on camera and talking) *not* to introduce Miss Canada but to bring on the girl singer instead. This sort of indecision can hardly be expected to help any show run smoothly.

Jarvis was in a ticklish position. Having insisted on King as his director, he felt obliged to give him a fairly free hand. Sometimes, he would step in and countermand King's orders but this only caused more confusion. While King was up in the control booth, Jarvis was on the studio floor and had audio communication with King. Naturally, they saw things from different viewpoints. If Jarvis disagreed with something King was doing, he'd say so on the intercom. But King had the responsibility of calling the shots. The pressure on him was tremendous; even a more seasoned director would have found it trying. That his shooting was erratic and his decisions sometimes confusing was almost inevitable under these conditions.

But the audience doesn't know all this—or care about it. All they see is the show—good, bad, indifferent, sloppy, uncertain, smooth, fumbling, enjoyable, irritating or whatever. Only the show matters. Audiences aren't interested in alibis, however valid they may be.

Some weeks after the show went on the air, Jarvis, King and I had a lunch meeting, the purpose of which was to "clear the air" and for Pat and myself to try to understand each other better in hopes of working together more smoothly. It was a pleasant lunch and a lively talk, but I don't know that it accomplished much.

The writers, too, had their grievances against both King and Jarvis. These concerned the basic and chronic conflict between producers or directors on the one hand and writers on the other: changes in a show being made without consultation with the writers. Jarvis was always pressing the writers to come up with ideas and suggestions for the show; yet, when they did, those ideas were often accepted and later ignored or changed.

Jarvis, on the other hand, had his beefs about the writers. He felt they weren't contributing enough to the show. He wanted them to be more aggressive, more inventive, more dynamic.

Our writing staff, incidentally, had undergone more changes. Alfie Scope, originally signed on as a researcher became more involved in the writing, or, at least, in contributing ideas. Des Hardman, a veteran ad agency man, was also added as a kind of consultant. At the same time, due to illness, Ken Gunton was taking an increasingly smaller part in the show.

King, meanwhile, continued to be negative. He was against booking Artie Shaw as a guest, maintaining that Shaw was "old hat." (He may have been old hat as a musician, but he's a fascinating conversationalist.) I knew of a nine-year-old boy who had the uncommon knack of being knowledgeable on horse racing—even to the extent of frequently picking winners—and who also had a sparkling, appealing personality. I felt he would be an interesting guest; King argued that this was "prostituting the show."

There was a continuing debate on the merits of an opening monologue, which I was doing each week. From the first, Starmer didn't like it. King didn't like it. Jarvis was uncertain. The writers and I felt it was important and that even though the results weren't always successful we should keep trying.

Added to these pressures and conflicts was the built-in uncertainty on this particular show: the uncertain length of time each week's show would last. We never knew beforehand if we'd have a thirty-minute show, or thirty-five or forty. We would be on the air live at the conclusion of the earlier hockey game, then welcome the rest of the network whenever the second game ended, and go for thirty minutes from that point.

I have gone into considerable detail about the background and conditions surrounding this series. This is intended to give the reader some idea of the labor pains of a new show. It is not intended as any apology, nor as a cop-out for the show's failure to survive. Despite the disagreements, despite the pressures, despite the sometimes harrowing conditions under which the show was put on, I don't happen to think an apology is called for. I'm not ashamed of the shows we did. I wasn't delighted over all of them, but I think some of them were good enough to justify my faith in the concept of the program.

Even before the first show in the series went on the air, we suffered another blow. We learned that we would be pre-empted for two successive Saturdays in October because of the Mexico City Olympics.

We were to start a new live show in September—before the hockey season started, which meant the bulk of that Saturday night audience would not be watching. We were to do three shows to the smaller audiences before hockey started. Then, the fourth week we would have the hockey audience. And right after that we'd be off the air for two weeks because of the Olympics. Then, we'd return and it would be like starting over again from scratch trying to build a following.

The CBC was committed to the program for only thirteen weeks, with options. As usual, the network would decide along about the ninth or tenth week whether the show would continue beyond thirteen weeks. We began, very much aware of the hurdles before us. The first three shows, as I've said, played to a small audience—and the critics. The fourth show, on October 12, marked the start of the hockey season and the presence of a much larger audience.

Our thoughts were on those two pre-emptions—two weeks off the air, so soon in the life of a new series. Bob Jarvis felt we needed a very strong fourth show to arouse enough interest to counteract the two-week layoff. He booked Hope Diamond, a well-known stripper. She did a rather tame strip tease and also chatted with me. We got some angry mail, but at least we were noticed. To that extent, she served her purpose.

Then, for our "return" three weeks later, we had booked Artie Shaw. This night, November 2, also marked a big night in hockey. The Montreal Forum had been closed until then for alterations. This was the night of the Forum's reopening and special festivities were planned which resulted in delaying the start of the Montreal game by some thirty-five minutes.

We went on the air at the end of the Toronto game, about ten-twenty. But since the Montreal game was so far behind, we ran for better than half an hour before the full network was joined—and then had to do thirty minutes from that point on. We did a show that ran about an hour and five minutes. In some ways it was our best show—partly because Shaw is such an interesting man to talk to, but also partly because the extended length gave us time to relax and let the show run its course instead of rushing to get everything in within the usual thirty to forty minutes.

Ironically, this show was also to prove our undoing. The delay in Montreal which caused us to run so long also delayed the CBC National News by some twenty minutes. We didn't know it then, but the news department, incensed that a mere variety show should delay the news, registered a complaint with the CBC brass.

Eugene Hallman, head of the English Networks Division, was sympathetic to the news department's complaint and quickly solved the matter: he simply decreed that this must not happen again. He didn't bother, however, communicating this decision to Bruce Raymond or Doug Nixon, the two men most directly involved with running the network, nor even to Len Starmer, supervisor of light entertainment. Naturally, nobody lower than that—like the producer, director or performers—was informed, either.

We learned about it—quite by accident—two weeks later. We discovered that if our program wasn't finished by eleven o'clock it was simply to be cut off the air at that time, even if I was in the middle of a word.

We learned this on a Saturday evening, a couple of hours before air time. We learned it the way you so often learn things around the CBC—by rumor. Jarvis was naturally furious when he checked the rumor and found it was true. He promptly telephoned Starmer and Nixon (Raymond was away) to complain. To his astonishment, neither of them knew anything about it.

As it happened, that night both games were over before ten-thirty and we were able to complete our half hour of full network show by eleven P.M. Thus, the order to cut us off the air didn't have to be enforced. Had it been, of course, the CBC would have had to face some angry sponsors, because the network was committed to providing for those sponsors a minimum of thirty minutes of our program on the full network.[1]

The following week, Raymond and Nixon were in Ottawa, presumably arguing with higher brass over this arbitrary and quite unrealistic ruling. By the next week, we were told the cut-off ruling had been rescinded.

It didn't occur to us then, but we should have realized this was the death knell. Obviously, the reason the order had been rescinded was that somewhere up there a decision had already been made to cancel the show in a few weeks, so the fuss over delaying of newscasts was pointless. But nobody said this. We were just told the order had been rescinded.

There had, in fact, already been rumors of a cancellation and I had gone to Starmer and asked about these rumors. He assured me he had heard of no such decision. He was fairly confident we would be extended beyond the thirteen weeks.

But the next week, the week of our eighth program, he indicated that "network" would be looking hard at that Saturday's show and that a decision on its future might be made after that. He also urged me to drop the monologue, that very week. I agreed to do so, not because I felt he was right but because I gathered from his tone that he felt this could be a factor in the network's decision about the show.

On that show, our guests included two prominent and somewhat unusual businessmen, Leon Weinstein, president of Loblaws, and Sam (Shopsy) Shopsowitz, the hot dog "king." Both are friends of mine, both are ardent amateur musicians, both are interesting and amusing. Because of their connection with the food industry, we had allowed for a question period, so that members of our studio audience could ask them about food prices, packaging, merchandising and the like.

The following Monday morning, Starmer called me at home and told me, regretfully, that Bruce Raymond had

---

[1] The following Friday night, I watched a college football game on the CBC. It ran long and delayed the National News by twenty-two minutes, but it was not cut off in mid-game. Variety may not be more important than news, but apparently football is.

made the decision to cancel the show. I asked him if this was final and he said it was. I then requested that the CBC make an immediate announcement to that effect, so as to avoid days or weeks of rumors, denials and all sorts of press speculation. I had long since learned that there is no way of keeping a secret around the CBC—someone invariably calls the press.

The announcement went out that afternoon and appeared in the next day's Toronto papers. It quoted Raymond as saying the program had "failed to live up to expectations." That sounds nice and tidy, but if you stop to examine it for a moment you'll see how empty it is. What expectations? What was it Raymond or Starmer or the CBC expected our program to be that it wasn't?

We had featured a few internationally known guests: Artie Shaw, Tammy Grimes, Arthur Hailey. We had presented some fine Canadian talent: Mary Lou Collins, the Sugar Shoppe, Sandra O'Neill, Diane Brooks, Bill Walker. We had offered informal conversation with such diverse people as Judy LaMarsh, Kontineta Horn, Stanley Burke, hockey badboy Howie Young and Charlie Chamberlain. We had employed some of Toronto's finest musicians under the leadership of trumpeter Guido Basso. We had been topical, light, occasionally controversial.

This, it seems to me, was more or less what we were "expected" to do. What expectations, then, had we failed to live up to? Smoothness and polish? These could come only with time. Ratings? An audience, too, takes time to build. We had been allowed eight shows—with a two-week interruption between the fourth and fifth—to build a following.

I thought about all this for a day or two, then decided I should seek a meeting with Bruce Raymond. I had no hopes of changing his mind, but I felt I was entitled to a better explanation of the cancellation than that vague reference to "expectations." My meeting with Raymond lasted almost four hours. It was, to me, a rather remarkable conversation.

Raymond told me, for example, with some pride that the ad agencies representing our sponsors had "torn the hide off" him for cancelling the show. In other words, the sponsors had in no way indicated any dissatisfaction with the show. (I was later able to confirm this through agency representatives.) What I marvelled at was Raymond's bragging, in effect, that he couldn't be intimidated by sponsors.

He told me that a few weeks before he had come "very close" to confirming our show for the full thirty-nine-week season in hopes such a vote of confidence would help us to "settle down." But he had not done that—he just came very close.

He told me he couldn't quite put his finger on what was wrong with the show, but the "chemistry" wasn't working. Each week, he said, there was something he didn't like—not always the same thing, he said, but always something.

He told me he was appalled that we had allowed such a "commercial plug" for Loblaws on the previous week's show. (That was our questions to Weinstein and Shopsy about food.)

He told me that I didn't seem "at ease." He said he didn't like the direction of the show, and that he didn't like Janet Baird.

He glossed over the matter of the conflict caused by the delaying of the news telecast, barely acknowledging that this had caused "some complications."

And he said that despite the CBC's determination not to be swayed by press criticism, he had to admit that "perhaps" the steady barrage of bricks thrown by one critic[1] had "influenced" him.

My answer to all these arguments (except for the last one) was that he had told me nothing that couldn't have been solved without killing the show. It could be taped, rather than live; it could be moved to a different time slot, to take the pressure off it; any director or performer who was considered inadequate could be replaced. He agreed with all this, he said, but it wasn't his job to "go down there and show them how to put on shows."

I repeated my faith in the idea of the show and my belief that there should be room in Canadian television for such a show. He agreed. I asked if he would give serious consideration to a proposal for continuing the show, perhaps in a dif-

---

[1] The critic in question was Patrick Scott of the Toronto *Star,* who never let a week go by without at least two or three reminders to his readers that he hated our show.

ferent time slot and with a reduced budget if necessary. He said yes, he definitely would. He suggested I discuss the idea with Starmer.

This I did, of course. Starmer said he couldn't believe Raymond was serious, but he agreed to check it out. He later said that Raymond had told him he might consider reviving the show "at some future time"—but not now.

And so, we were to wind up Barris & Company on December 28, at the end of the thirteenth show.

Incredibly enough, after having decided to kill our show, the Corporation suddenly discovered it really had no idea what to put in its place. There was talk of a Montreal show, or of one from Vancouver.

Montreal was given the nod (a then local show called "Comedy Café" was to be put on the network in the latest attempt to solve the Saturday night problem) but it soon developed Montreal wasn't quite ready to take over.

So it was decided to extend our show for another few weeks to give the Montreal program time to prepare its replacement. And even before that show went on the air (February first) the CBC had already decided it was no good for more than six weeks, and yet another show was being prepared in Toronto to replace the replacement.

Anyone in television knows that one of the most difficult things to do is to continue a program for several weeks after you've been told it's to be cancelled. In our case, the axe fell after we had done our eighth show. But we did not expire until we had done nine more shows—a total of seventeen, more than half of them after the decision to cancel had been announced.

We continued to present some outstanding guests—Tommy Hunter, Eartha Kitt, Barbara Hamilton, the Irish Rovers, Robert Goulet and Joyce Sullivan, Larry Mann, Gordie Tapp, Paul Kligman, Oscar Peterson, Betty Robertson, Alan Crofoot. And, not surprisingly, our ratings improved steadily. In my marathon talk with Raymond I had argued that no program I could think of had ever proven itself in eight weeks. He agreed, but the decision had been made.

From the beginning we were doing slightly better than In Person, our predecessor, had done. By November (in fact, a few days before Raymond made his momentous decision) our ratings were fairly respectable. By mid-December, we were getting bigger audiences than Quentin Durgens, MP, and the public affairs department's The Way It Is. By the end of that month, we were only slightly behind the Tommy Hunter Show, one of the CBC's most popular programs. We were reaching close to three million Canadians.

This knowledge made it that much more difficult to go on each week, knowing that the program was doomed—despite all the logical reasons for continuing it. It is one of those awful times when you suddenly realize the truth of that most tired of all show business clichés—the one about the show having to go on.

All things considered, I guess we got through those nine weeks pretty well. The day we learned of the cancellation was difficult. That night, some of us connected with the program got together and tied one on. This resulted in some monumental hangovers. But I shouldn't complain about that —I firmly believe that a hangover is one of the few things in life that no one gets without earning it.

The following Saturday, we started the show with a cold opening (a one-line blackout, prior to the identification of the program) that we felt struck the proper note of irreverence. Maggie St. Clair stood in front of a camera and said: "I'll tell you how to end the war in Viet Nam. Send Alex Barris over there and the war will be cancelled in thirteen weeks."

In the weeks following, I found it fairly easy (at least while we were actually doing the shows) to forget about our depression and simply have fun on the shows. Jarvis and others connected with the show commented that I was coming through more relaxed now. This was natural enough; the pressure was off, whatever happened on the show could result in no more severe punishment than the one we'd already been given. I kept remembering Raymond's comment that he had come "very close" to confirming the continuation of the show—for this very reason, to lessen the pressure.

The only thing that put me off was the ill-disguised sympathy of our make-up girl. She felt so sorry for me that she kept looking at me as if I had terminal cancer. But she was a dear girl and she meant well. Only on the day of the last show did I feel really depressed. The day seemed to drag on endlessly. I wanted it over with. But the hours passed, we did our show, and that was it. The series was over—seventeen weeks from start to finish.

Our show had not been the greatest. I don't kid myself that it was even as good as I had hoped it would be. But I think there was enough evidence in the seventeen weeks that it could have developed into what we started out to do. I believed then, and still do, that had it been given a full season it would have proven itself and been renewed for another season.

I still believe there is a place on the CBC for this sort of show—call it imitation of Carson or Griffin, or whatever you like: an informal talk show, interspersed with variety entertainment, on which Canadian personalities can be seen and heard in a context and atmosphere in which they can register as human beings, with ideas, with humor, with opinions.

Part of my regret that the show went off is that I know from experience that it will be that much longer, now, before anyone at the CBC tries such a show again. It took me the better part of two years to talk the CBC into doing it this time. It certainly won't be me next time. I learned years ago —and stated in an earlier chapter—that what is needed to get a show on the air is someone in a position of power to have faith in the idea of the show; and that what brings about its demise is that nobody in such a position has faith in it any longer.

However Bruce Raymond or anyone else in the CBC defines it, however I may try to rationalize it—this is exactly what happened again. The CBC lost faith in the program, or in me, or in the combination of me and the program. Perhaps they were right in doing so. Obviously, I don't think so. I can't claim objectivity in the matter.

Who Reads the Critics?

That anyone who has been involved in television should touch on the subject of critics is bound to appear suspect in some quarters.

The writer, director or performer is not supposed to comment on critics. He is supposed to sit back, unruffled and dignified, and mouth mealy sentiments like, "I welcome constructive criticism . . . or "I never read reviews."

Of course, such statements don't ring true when uttered by anybody who has, at one time or another, been impaled by a critic. But, no matter—many people in show business make these statements, anyway.

Then, there is the other extreme. The actor or artist suddenly given a forum from which to strike back at critics sometimes can't resist being as abusive as the critic had been in his review.

You know all those clichés about critics—the critic is like a eunuch; he sees the trick done every night but he can't do it himself . . . a critic is a legless man who teaches running, and so on.

I don't happen to agree with that view, any more than I agree with the theory that "those who can, do; those who can't, teach."

First of all, there are too many examples of critics who also have made creative contributions to the arts for that "eunuch" definition to be taken very seriously.

Walter Kerr, the drama critic of the New York *Times* and one of the most highly regarded of American critics, has also directed in the theatre and written several books on theatre.

Kenneth Tynan, before he began a more active role in the theatre in England, was one of the most articulate and knowledgeable of theatre critics, both in England and America.

Harold Clurman, who has produced and directed works by all the leading playwrights, is also a widely respected drama critic.

Wolcott Gibbs, the late critic of the *New Yorker*, was also a successful playwright, as was another of his colleagues, William Archer. Edmund Wilson, a towering figure in American literary criticism, has also written novels, poetry and essays.

In Canada, to name only a couple of examples, Herbert Whittaker, drama critic of the *Globe and Mail*, has both directed and designed many theatrical productions. And Mavor Moore, author, producer, director and actor, has also worked as a drama critic.

Perhaps the most convincing example of all is that of George Bernard Shaw, who was an excellent music critic before he became a playwright.

No one would claim that all critics can reach the creative heights, but I think there is enough evidence that critics are not necessarily all embittered men who tear down that which they envy.

It is true there are not enough good critics, not enough of them qualified to appraise intelligently the creations or performances of artists. But then, too, there are never enough great artists.

The point I'm making is that I am certainly not "anti-critic." I couldn't be, anyway. I have worked both sides of the street. During my newspaper years, I wrote film criticism, as well as some theatrical and television criticism. On more than one occasion, I have been involved in debates, mostly on radio or TV talk shows, about the "value" or the "role" of criticism. Often, I have been in the position of trying to defend critics—at least those in Toronto.

As it happens, Toronto seems to have gained some sort of reputation as a "tough" city, with regard to its critics. David Merrick, that publicity-conscious Broadway producer, never misses a chance to knock critics, knowing full well that the newspapers will faithfully print every word of his attacks rather than be accused of suppressing criticism of the critics.

He says that Toronto critics are the worst. He says that,

mind you, when he is in Toronto. When he's in Cleveland, he says Cleveland's critics are the worst, and so on. He is always reported—thus his shows get more publicity than they might otherwise.

Merrick's pose is completely phoney. He complains that critics give his shows bad reviews—which is not always true. He also says that all critics, indeed all newspapers, are "crooked." Critics, he maintains, can be "bought" for a bottle of whisky. But if he believed that, the solution would be simple. To a man who spends hundreds of thousands of dollars to produce a show, the cost of a few bottles of whisky to assure favorable reviews would be a simple detail. Funny that he's never tried it.

Merrick is not alone. Another top Broadway producer, Herman Levin, who had produced *My Fair Lady*, brought a later musical to Toronto. It was rejected by the Toronto critics. Levin then made a speech to a service club (fully reported by the press) denouncing the Toronto critics and advising them to study the work of New York critics to learn how to do their jobs. His show next opened in New York— where the critics were equally unimpressed with it. The show folded, but there is no record of Mr. Levin's having acknowledged the accuracy of the Toronto critics—nor, incidentally, of his repeating his earlier praise for the New York critics.

Theatre operators also tend to damn the critics, whose comments on a play or film can affect their business. When I was reviewing movies for the *Globe and Mail*, some years back, the then advertising manager of that newspaper was forever complaining that my "tough" reviews were causing theatre owners to cut down the amount of advertising they placed in the paper.

This was nonsense, of course. To begin with, I wasn't a very "tough" critic. But more to the point, the reason that the theatres advertised more in the afternoon papers than in the *Globe and Mail*, a morning paper, was that the theatre operators had long since learned that an ad in an afternoon paper was of more value to them. (Morning papers usually "go out" of the home, being taken by the husband when he leaves for work; afternoon papers "come in" to the home, where the wife—who usually chooses what movie she and her husband will see—has all afternoon to look over the ads.)

Like most people, I have my own ideas about what a critic is for and what he should do. I believe, first of all, that the critic must love the subject on which he writes—be it art, literature, theatre, music, films, television or whatever. This does not mean he must praise everything that comes along; on the contrary, the more he loves the art form, the more demanding he is likely to be that it meet certain standards. By way of balance, it should be added, that love will tend to make him tolerant of minor shortcomings, encouraging rather than obstructing growth and improvement.

I do not believe a critic can be "objective." What he writes is opinion, judgment, appraisal—not simple, dispassionate reportage of fact. There are producers and theatre owners who would prefer the latter—such and such a play opened last night, there were so many people present, the audience applauded so many times, et cetera — but no attempt at all to evaluate the play, the production or the performances.

But this, of course, is nonsense because it fails to do precisely what the critic is expected to do. The critic, I feel, should serve as a guide to the public. Such a guide is, if not an absolute necessity, at last a useful service. If you go to buy a car, you are allowed to test drive it. If you buy a suit, you can try it on first. If some appliance or item of clothing is no good, you can return it and get a refund.

But there is no way of test-driving a play, or trying on a movie. You read the ads, which invariably exaggerate the merits of the play or movie, and then take a gamble. If you don't like it, if the ad was misleading, you can't ask for your money back. The critic, therefore, can serve as a guide—a counter-balance to the claims of the advertiser. With no axe to grind, he is in a position to tell you whether that new show is as good as the ads say. Since part of the newspaper's traditional role is to serve the public, this is a part of that service.

I do not believe that a critic is particularly useful to those creating or producing shows. True, now and then a critic may make a point that a producer might find helpful in improving his show. More often than not, however, the critic's suggestions have already been considered and probably abandoned for some reason (technical, financial, et cetera) the critic isn't aware of. The point is, the critic's primary function is to help guide the public—not the showman. Too many critics tend to lose sight of this.

Of course, what the critic says is his opinion. He must try to be fair, to avoid being swayed by either friendships or enmities; but his evaluation of any production, creation or performance must be partly subjective—he can only judge by how the show affected his emotions or evoked some response from him. Nevertheless, the critic's opinion is regarded as an expert opinion, worth a bit more than the opinion of the average consumer. His background, training, experience and understanding of the art he is criticizing give his opinion this added weight. To deny this is to deny the validity of "experts" in any field.

How much attention should the public pay to critics? Well, the critic is a human being—subject to tastes, likes, dislikes, preferences, even prejudices. All the reader can do is "sample" the critics: read this one for a while, then try another. In time, the reader will find the critic whose interests, tastes and standards approximate his own. Thus, the reader will have found the "best" critic for him—the one whose guidance he can believe in and trust and follow.

From the newspaper's standpoint, other qualities are desirable in a critic: that he be able to write lucidly, knowledgeably, freely and entertainingly. He must be able to write in a way that readers will understand; he should be versed in the field of activity he is appraising; he must be free to voice his opinions; and he must keep the newspaper's readers interested.

This last thing, unfortunately, can create its own problems. There are critics, in every field and in many cities, who attach more importance (perhaps because their newspapers do) to being entertaining, or provocative, or controversial, than to being valid and responsible.[1]

In some instances, it is the personality of the critic through

---

[1] The Toronto *Star's* Nathan Cohen, a pioneer in the field of sensational criticism, likes to claim publicly that he is Canada's only critic. Herbert Whittaker, the *Globe and Mail's* critic, was once asked by a broadcaster to comment on this claim. Said Whittaker: "Nathan may not be our only dramatic critic, but he is certainly our most dramatic critic."

his writing that attracts readers rather than the validity of his criticism. The temptation, particularly for neophytes, to establish a reputation sometimes overrides other considerations. The critic uses the art he is supposed to appraise as a canvas for his own wit or "style."

A good example of this was John McCarten, for many years the film critic for the *New Yorker*. McCarten's writing always had an edge to it; his "reviews" consistently ridiculed the films he wrote about. His writing was anything but dull. But his value as a critic was negligible, because he was not concerned with guiding his readers, with honest evaluation of the film at hand—only with exhibiting his own wit.

I believe that a critic has certain responsibilities, not only to his newspaper but to his readers. One of these is honesty. If he truly considers that the play or film in question is on the whole a failure, I believe it is dishonest for him to seek out the few good qualities to emphasize while ignoring the faults. By the same token, I believe that if a work is on the whole successful, it is just as dishonest that the critic should seek out and magnify its minor shortcomings while ignoring its merits.

There are critics who do not use any such guidelines. One obvious reason for this is the temptation to be "different," to establish a reputation for "toughness," to be talked about, to attract attention to themselves and their clever writing.

Another and equally disturbing reason is a kind of mental laziness. I know from experience that it is far easier to write an unfavorable review than a favorable one. It is a relatively simple matter to find imperfections in any production and bring attention to them, magnify them, ridicule them. It requires somewhat more thought and work to convey to the reader what is worthwhile about a production, why it deserves his support. The critic who sees as his primary function the need to be read and talked about knows instinctively that he can achieve that goal far more easily by knocking than by praising. And there has yet to be a play or film or book or work of music that was absolutely perfect, completely free of flaws if one wanted to find flaws.[1]

Every collection of witty quotations includes some by

---

[1] I once wanted Larry Mann to do an imitation of Nathan Cohen reviewing the second coming of Christ—and panning it as "predictable."

critics. It is no accident that these are always unfavorable comments. The devastating one-liners ("She ran the gamut of emotions from A to B"; "So-and-so played the King and lost") are quoted, savored, talked about, included in anthologies of wit. I defy you to find any quotation in these books from a critic's favorable review; you cannot, because words of praise for a Hamlet or a Haydn are not assembled in pungent, quotable sentences, nor spiced with insult.

Earlier, I cited some examples of critics whose credentials must be respected by virtue of their own creative contributions to the arts. Such involvement or experience in the arts is, of course, helpful to a critic—not only because it equips him to better understand and appreciate the artistic endeavors of others, but also because it gives him added stature in the eyes of his reading public. I don't mean to suggest that it is absolutely necessary that a critic should have worked, at some time, in the particular art form of which he writes. This is not often possible. A large metropolitan daily newspaper is in a better position, naturally, to employ as critics men with some such background and experience. Papers in smaller centres are much less likely to be so fortunate.

Still, critics, like other journalists, are made rather than born. A young reporter may start by covering the courts, then be assigned to city hall, move up to the provincial legislature, and then be appointed the paper's Ottawa correspondent. There is logic to such a sequence—the background and experience in the earlier stages help to train the reporter to cover the larger arena of federal government activities.

Similarly, the young reporter in the sports department of a paper will first be assigned to school games, then gradually move up to cover the big leagues. Thus, over a period of time, he becomes something of an authority in the field he is covering. He needn't have been a jockey to write of horse racing—but he must watch many races, talk to jockeys and trainers, soak up the atmosphere, learn the rules, know the tricks.

It would seem logical, therefore, that a critic should serve some sort of apprenticeship before becoming a full-fledged critic—possibly starting with amateur theatricals and then moving up. During this apprenticeship, the editor has a chance to observe the writer's special interests and talents, so that he may be steered towards the field of criticism for which he is best suited.

But when we come to television criticism, this doesn't often seem to be the practice. Perhaps it cannot be. The television critic must, after all, have a broad and varied background and interests. He is being asked to judge drama, music, comedy, variety, sports, news coverage, public affairs, documentaries, film direction and production, dance, playwriting, acting—plus a whole new medium of communication called television, which has its own techniques and style.

That's a pretty tall order and you would think the editors of a newspaper would think long and hard before choosing the man to cope with it. But that, alas, is not always the case. And there are reasons for it—not necessarily acceptable reasons, but reasons nevertheless. To understand them, one must know something of the newspaper philosophy.

To the everlasting shame of the majority of newspapers on this continent, the history of newspaper coverage of radio—especially in its earlier years—is deplorable. Too many newspapers adopted the ostrich-like pose of ignoring radio in hopes it would go away. Radio was, after all, "competition," and it simply was not considered good business to attract attention to one's rival. Many newspapers refused to write anything about radio activities—in the days when such activities involved substantially more than the spinning of records and the reading of news bulletins. Many refused even to list the daily schedules of radio programming, for this, too, constituted giving aid and comfort to the enemy.

The publishers and editors felt they were justified in such a stand. Radio was competing with newspapers by giving news; more important, it was accepting advertising, which simply meant that the advertiser was being tempted to spend his money in radio instead of newspapers.

What the newspapers chose to ignore was that the newspaper traditionally is more than a business, more than merely another moneymaking enterprise. The newspaper has a responsibility to the public, to the community it is supposed to serve. That responsibility is to report, to keep the community aware of everything of significance and interest that is going on. And if that includes theatre, books, films, sports and other forms of recreation and/or entertainment, then, of course, it must include radio when radio was added to the list of diversions available to the public. The newspaper cannot arbitrarily ignore an area of activity simply because of its own business interests.

In time, some of the better newspapers recognized the foolishness of their attitude and acknowledged the existence of radio. Others never did.

When television came along—with at least the same impact radio had had a quarter of a century before—the newspapers were again confronted with this dilemma: must a newspaper bring attention to this healthy new rival, thus perhaps risking the hastening of its own demise? Did the newspaper's responsibility to the public demand coverage of television, or could it be ignored?

Again, some newspapers tried to pretend that television wasn't there. In some papers there were even internal conflicts on this matter.

When television began in Canada, I was working at the *Globe and Mail*. I was writing a daily column which included movie reviews and entertainment news generally. The editor under whom I worked felt that some recognition of the existence of television was called for and wanted some coverage of it included in my column. But he was opposed in this by the newspaper's advertising manager.

This man, who was responsible for bringing in the paper's revenue, felt it was an affront to movie theatre advertisers to bring attention to a medium that was in direct competition with movies. Also, he was aware that as television grew it would begin to draw advertising dollars away from the newspaper. This conflict between the two departments within a newspaper—the classic conflict that always exists in every newspaper and must constantly be kept in check—eventually prompted me to leave the *Globe and Mail*.[1]

On the whole, the larger newspapers wasted less time in recognizing the existence of television than they had with radio. Despite the competition for advertisers, most newspapers bravely faced up to the fact that TV was here to stay—

---

[1] The *Telegram* offered me a place there and I accepted, not because the offer was so attractive but because the situation at the *Globe and Mail* had become untenable.

and that newspaper readers were interested in knowing all about it.

This didn't happen overnight. But after a little magazine called *TV Guide* rapidly built a staggeringly high circulation (some twelve million a week, second only to the *Readers' Digest*) thus proving that readers were interested in TV news, it was amazing how many newspapers hopped on the bandwagon and began turning out their own local imitations of *TV Guide*.

But covering television doesn't always mean covering it fairly. If that sounds like a terrible accusation, please remember that newspapers had abundant reason to be opposed to TV—partly because the new medium was siphoning off advertising dollars. But also for another, perhaps less obvious reason.

I don't think it's an exaggeration to say that most newspapers were and are opposed to the CBC—opposed to its very existence. This shouldn't be surprising. After all, the CBC represents to most businessmen a kind of negation of the free enterprise system. It is publicly financed, government owned and operated. Newspaper publishers are, among other things, businessmen. That they should be against this form of crypto-socialism is understandable.

This attitude is reflected, again and again, in editorials that cry out for curbs on the CBC's powers, tighter reins on its budgets, and often even phasing out of the publicly owned corporation in favor of privately owned broadcasting stations and networks.

The CBC has been subjected to this kind of opposition for all the years of its existence. It isn't terribly difficult, it seems, to whip up a fair amount of public indignation by harping on how much the CBC costs the taxpayers of this country.

Just as most politicians know that the way to get elected is to strike out at government spending and to vow they will cut down that spending, newspaper publishers know they satisfy a lot of people by taking the same stand. It's not even necessary to suggest the publishers do this cynically—they really feel that way, they really would rather see private television replace the CBC and thus cut down on taxation.

But there is some cynicism involved, too. Whether or not

the taxpayers stop to think about it, businessmen (including newspaper publishers) are shrewd enough to know that this argument is specious. True enough, eliminating or even curbing the CBC will cut down taxes. But that doesn't mean television would be "free." All it means is that the money to pay for it would be extracted from the public in a different way.

Private broadcasters must make money (or, at least, not lose money) in order to stay in business. So they aren't going to pay for the programs. They will charge the sponsors. But sponsors, being businessmen, also have to show a profit. So they aren't going to lose money on TV shows. What they do is simply add the cost of advertising—TV, newspapers, or any other kind—onto the price of their product. So it's still the public, the same taxpayer, who will pay. The only difference is that instead of paying it to the government in taxes he pays it in the price of soap, gasoline, cigarets, cars, shampoos, toothpaste and all the other products advertised by sponsors who "pay" for television programs.

But the newspaper publisher doesn't care about this. He still doesn't like the CBC because he, like every other businessman, has to pay the taxes to subsidize it. He would much rather eliminate the taxes and let you, the TV viewer, pay for your television entertainment by subsidizing the manufacture of deodorants or frozen foods.

Thus, it should not be surprising to find the tone of much television coverage in our press regularly anti-CBC. That it is also sometimes incompetent, inaccurate and shallow is the result of the "system" often used in selecting people from the staffs of newspapers to be appointed as TV critics—overnight experts in the most dynamic medium of communication of our time.

The fact is there is no "system." An editor or publisher looks around for a bright, clever writer—one who can attract and entertain readers. That he may never have read or seen a play (much less have written one), that he may be tone deaf, that he may have no knowledge of the background or techniques of television or the people in it, that he may have narrow intellectual horizons, that he may be culturally a peasant—such considerations don't often seem to enter into it.

I'm not charging that every television critic is so patently unqualified—but some are. I'm not suggesting that editors deliberately go out of their way to choose the most inept reporters for such jobs—but in some cases they might just as well.

Of course, some critics grow into their jobs. But part of the problem is that newspapers generally don't consider the coverage of television as having any importance (except where that coverage deals with the political or financial aspects of the CBC, or with any blunder or bit of scandal that can be used to embarrass the CBC); nor do they consider it important that a critic have any special background or training for his role. In the smaller communities, this is understandable. The editors there can't be too fussy in selecting potential critics from their staffs. This has been so, incidentally, not only with regard to television, but to films and theatre as well. But in the metropolitan areas, there is less reason for such a potluck method of assigning reporters to become daily judges of the merits of television programming.

But it is not simply the availability of qualified people that determines the appointment of TV critics. It is the belief that what matters most to the reader is that the critic be entertaining and provocative—which often means abusing, ridiculing or dismissing the bulk of television fare, especially if it emanates from that huge and traditional target of Canadian newspapers—the CBC.

This is far more obvious, of course, in situations where a newspaper publisher has an axe to grind, a special interest to be served. In Toronto, for example, John Bassett, publisher of the *Telegram,* is also the owner of CFTO-TV, the privately-owned television channel and the dominant station of the CTV network.[1]

For a number of years, the television critic of the *Telegram* was Bob Blackburn, whose job it evidently was to downgrade most CBC efforts while puffing up everything CFTO-TV did as significant and/or magnificent.

---

[1] Mr. Bassett is certainly not alone in this. Among others who have substantial financial interests in both newspapers or magazines and broadcasting outlets are K. C. Irving and Geoff Stirling in the Maritimes, the Davies and Blackburn families in Ontario, Max Bell of Calgary, Maclean-Hunter, and the Sifton and Southam chains in various parts of Canada. In Canada's twenty largest centres, representing about half of the country's population, newspaper and broadcasting interests are interlocking.

During some of these same years, by the way, the television critic for the rival Toronto *Star* was Roy Shields who, somehow, never did find much space in his column to write about (let alone praise) the activities of CFTO-TV. But late in 1968, Blackburn was relieved of his duties and Shields moved from the *Star* to the *Telegram*. Amazingly, Shields suddenly found the day-to-day activities of CFTO-TV infinitely more interesting and praiseworthy than while he had been at the *Star*.

One need not look always for ulterior motives. Baiting the CBC has long been an accepted practice for newspapers—and particularly for TV critics on newspapers. When Juliette's program was dropped by the CBC, you could have launched an aircraft carrier in the tears shed by TV critics all across Canada. Yet in her ten years on the air the overwhelming majority of the critics had not a kind word for her. They hated her smile, they called her corny, square, gushy, sentimental, insincere, old-fashioned. When her program was dropped, suddenly many of these same critics came to the conclusion that she wasn't so bad—or, more to the point, that whatever replaced her program was worse. "Bring back Juliette," they cried. And I have no doubt that when and if the CBC decides to heed their advice, they will soon get right back into the old habit of knocking her—and the CBC for reinstating her.

Early in 1969, the CBC cancelled a scheduled drama on the Festival series and substituted a BBC film about Isadora Duncan, the colorful dancer of the 1920s. I happened to see the film and considered it an outstanding show. It was written, produced and directed by Ken Russell, regarded as one of the more exciting directors in Britain. But the next day, the press reacted predictably: one critic dismissed the program as "a fourth-rate BBC film" and another said it was noteworthy only because of a few shots of bare bosoms. Both critics devoted the bulk of their columns to reviling the CBC for being cowardly enough to cancel the scheduled drama because it was controversial. (No doubt, if the drama had been aired the same critics would have found it vulgar and worthless.)

I don't doubt that some TV critics would dismiss any comments I might make about their writings, on the grounds that I am merely striking back at critics who were tough on me. I have no intention of arguing with their opinions. But it's interesting how transparent their anti-CBC bias can be sometimes.

In the Vancouver *Sun*, TV critic Les Wedman began his review of the first Barris & Company show this way:

"Barris & Company is the first TV show I've ever seen where members of the studio audience walked out. Actually, there were only two; the show was over, but CBC cameras were still trying to record a favorable crowd reaction to Alex Barris' new variety program when the exodus began. . . ."

If Wedman had taken the trouble to look a bit more carefully instead of hurrying to jot down this bon mot, he might have noticed that the two persons involved in the "exodus" were wearing identical blazers. They were in fact ushers who had been sitting down watching the show and were now required to resume their posts at the rear of the aisles in order to guide the spectators out of the studio at the end of the show.

But why need a critic bother with such trivia? Much better—far wittier—to start off a review with the suggestion that the show was so bad the audience couldn't wait to get out.

Perhaps this is a picayune example. Let me tell you a little of the Toronto press "coverage" of Barris & Company.

Of the three papers, the Toronto *Star* came off best, at least from the standpoint of thoroughness. That's paper's TV critic (elevated to the position, by the way, only a couple of months before our program started) was Patrick Scott. He absolutely hated the show—he hated it before it started, he hated it when he first saw it, he continued to hate it— and said so quite clearly during its seventeen-week life. According to clippings which I have seen, Scott wrote about the program no less than in twenty-seven different columns during that period.[1] I did not find his comments especially pleasing, but I must acknowledge that he did indeed cover the program.

The *Telegram's* attitude was rather different. On Saturday,

---

[1]Scott reached what might be regarded as the height of his talent for constructive criticism the week we had singer Mary Lou Collins on the show. He wrote: "I'd been wondering for months who it was that Mary Lou Collins reminded me of, and now I know—Dustin Hoffman."

September 21, 1968, the day our series was to start—but before the program had been on the air—that newspaper ran a 2,500-word article on the front page of its entertainment section. The story was written by Bob Blackburn, the paper's TV critic, and a girl named Pat Johnson.

Apart from being riddled with distortions and inaccuracies (Sample: the article said the budget of the Tommy Hunter Show was $25,000 a week—this is only an exaggeration of slightly more than 100 per cent) the Blackburn-Johnson collaboration tried very hard to convey that the new show I was heading was of great importance, because there was so little variety entertainment in the CBC schedule. "Right now," it began, "what Alex Barris needs is the biggest pair of feet in show business." Anyone reading the article could hardly avoid the conclusion that the entire future of CBC variety programming rested on my shoulders.

This was a lot of bull, of course, but Blackburn and Miss Johnson had a perfect right to say it if they chose. However, you would think that a program of such earth-shaking significance would merit a review in the following Monday's paper. Did it get one? It did not. Not that Monday, or Tuesday, or Wednesday, or any other day that week, or the next week, or the next.

What was of profound importance a few hours before it went on the air was apparently now not even worth judging. Blackburn finally got around to reviewing the program on November fourth—a full six weeks later. His review might be described as grudgingly tolerant. "I wouldn't go out of my way to see it, but it was no strain at all to watch," he wrote. And this: "It's a mediocre show, perhaps, but it certainly wasn't bad."

That leaves the *Globe and Mail*. If there are people who read only this newspaper and no other—and I'm sure there must be some in Toronto—those people must have been a bit puzzled by the devotion to duty of one Leslie Millin, who "covers" television for the *Globe and Mail*.

On September 12, in the course of writing about a preview program produced by the CBC (a program announcing in some detail the network's fall schedule) Millin devoted some forty words to the new show called Barris & Company. This was nine days before we went on the air.

On November 26, the CBC announced it was cancelling the program—an item Millin found of sufficient interest to print.

During the ten weeks in between, Millin printed not one word about the program—not an opinion, not a review, not an item, not a hint, not a word. Thus does the *Globe and Mail's* critic "cover" television. At least some of that paper's readers must have wondered at news of the cancellation of a program about which their paper had told them nothing while it was on.

It's true that a good many critics in Canadian newspapers didn't like Barris & Company and said so. It is also true, however, that the ratings indicated that quite a few of the viewers disagreed with the critics—more and more of them were watching the program each week. And I know that the sponsors, while not deliriously happy with the show, were certainly content to go on sponsoring it.

Who, then, did the critics influence? The CBC, of course. And this is the most ludicrous part of it all.

I don't suggest for a moment that any critic should be prevented from saying what he wishes about any show. Nor would I urge the public to ignore the critics. The critic is there, after all, to guide the public, to give his informed opinion of whatever he is reviewing. It follows that those readers who believe in a particular critic will be influenced by the critic's opinions. Fine. But I do not believe that those people engaged in the business of creating entertainment—be they writers of plays, or actors, or film directors, or theatrical producers, or television executives—should spend too much time worrying about the critics.

Most people in show business know more about their business than the critics do. That's as it should be, just as the critics should know more about how to write for newspapers than theatrical producers do. It is natural that anyone in show business, from actor to network executive, likes to get favorable press notices. But he isn't in business to please critics, any more than the critic is in business to please producers. It is depressing that the CBC—knowing that the majority of the press is prejudiced against the CBC—should pay much attention to critics. It betrays, again, a lack of confidence by the CBC in its own abilities.

I think the point can be illustrated by an incident. Some years ago, Bette Davis and Gary Merrill (her husband at the time) toured with a stage production based on readings of Carl Sandburg's works. The show played in Toronto, on its way to Broadway.

One night after a performance in Toronto, Miss Davis and Mr. Merrill were guests of honor at a small party given by some well-to-do theatre patrons. I happened to be there, as was a senior editor of the *Telegram*, which was then publishing my column. At the time, Mavor Moore was working as theatre critic for the paper and he had found considerable fault with this particular production.

At the party, the editor in question was introduced to Gary Merrill. The editor mentioned Mavor Moore's review and suggested to Merrill that it might be worthwhile for Merrill to "get together" with Moore to discuss the latter's criticism. Merrill declined to pursue the conversation, turning to speak to some other guests. The editor became annoyed and pressed the point.

"Listen," he said, "our critic, Mavor Moore, has had a lot of experience. Don't you think it would be a good idea to have a meeting with him and get his suggestions on how you can improve your show?"

Merrill lost his cool. "No damn it, I don't," he said. "What the hell do you think we do—throw this kind of production together in a couple of days? This show represents considerable work on the part of many professionals. Whether you or your critic like it, this show is pretty well the way we think it should be. And we have no intention of running around the country changing it to suit the tastes or whims of every drama critic."

I felt like applauding Gary Merrill. I still do. I think his attitude was one that might well be considered seriously by many more people in show business—the CBC included.

The point is that in the final analysis, the person responsible for a show—the writer or the producer or the star or the network, or all of them—must go on instinct, judgment and taste of his (or their) own. He must apply his skill and experience and come up with the best show he is capable of doing. If the public likes it, fine; if not, too bad. But whether or not the critics like it is a matter of concern to the critic and to the public—not to the artist.

Let the critics write or not write; let them say what they will; let them pan or praise, ridicule or needle, ignore or applaud. Let them be. Let them do their thing. Read it, clip it out, curse it, save it, tear it up—but don't be ruled by it. Critics are supposed to write for the public—not the artists. And artists are supposed to do shows for the public, not the critics.

One day, maybe the CBC will come to understand this. Maybe. But I wouldn't want to hold my breath while I'm waiting.

Politics and Broadcasting

In the course of writing this book, I've had occasion to discuss parts of it with various people involved in television. When I've mentioned some of the points I planned to cover—and some of them might be described as unflattering to the CBC—I've been asked what I thought the CBC's "reaction" might be. I'm aware that some people will be annoyed or embarrassed or possibly infuriated by something or other in this book. And I know, too, that there's always a chance that some statements will be quoted out of context, a practice which can result in distorting the overall viewpoint of a book.

So, let me make it clear now: it is not my intention or wish that anything in this book should lead anyone to the conclusion that I am "against" the CBC or "angry" with it, or that I would like to see the CBC abolished, curbed, emasculated, replaced by private television, or detoured from its basic responsibility for providing a national broadcasting service for Canadians. If I find fault with it, the fault is there to be found, in my opinion. If I urge reforms, improvements, changes in attitude, I do so in the fervent belief that such reforms and improvements will strengthen the CBC and enable it to function more successfully. What has been apparent to me and others deeply involved in television for the past ten or twelve years is becoming increasingly obvious to many: the Pierce-Arrow Showroom is leaking and nobody seems to be on duty.

Considering that there have been two Royal Commissions and God knows how many lesser investigations into the CBC in the past decade, it might seem presumptuous for me to be discussing ways and means of improving the CBC. Maybe it is, but it's impossible to spend twelve years involved in any kind of work without arriving at some conclusions about it. At least, it's impossible for me.

In this chapter, therefore, I propose to point out some areas where I think changes or improvements are called for. These are my own views and I don't doubt some, both inside and outside the CBC, will disagree with them. But these opinions are not whims hastily arrived at or easily shaken.

The first problem, perhaps the most important, is also the most difficult to solve. Public broadcasting in Canada is and has long been a political football. Perhaps this is inevitable, simply because the CBC operates with public funds and therefore everyone feels entitled to have a say in how the funds are spent.

When I talk of politics in broadcasting, I'm not primarily concerned here with the periodic charges that the party in power uses, or used, the CBC as a propaganda arm. This may occasionally be true, but I have noticed that the Conservatives, who usually charge the Liberals with such a dastardly practice, were not always above indulging in it themselves when they were in power. Both have sometimes been guilty of this, and I know no sure cure for it, except for everyone to scream whenever it happens, thus possibly causing the culprits of the moment to resist the temptation.

I am more concerned with the influence politicians have in shaping the life, the existence, the activities, the finances of the CBC—not so much by injecting their political philosophies into CBC programming, but by controlling the quality and quantity of its activities and its facilities. It is a sad fact that he who pays the piper and thus feels entitled to call the tune is often tone-deaf.

It may be shrewd of a member of Parliament to ingratiate himself with his constituents by chipping away at the CBC, by slashing its budgets, by ridiculing its efforts, by inhibiting its freedom and even by applying pressure to influence its decisions. But such grandstand plays for the voters back home do nothing to improve broadcasting in Canada. It may be clever of a politician to wheel and deal, to support the government in exchange for some material handout, such as a new CBC building in his constituency. But neither is this likely to do much for the betterment of Canadian broadcasting. I recognize, of course, that politicians have a certain responsibility to those who elected them. But it would be nice if politicians could sometimes remember that they are in Ottawa to represent not only those local voters but the best interests of Canada as a whole. (You see, even cynical old newspapermen are capable of idealistic thoughts.)

Without wishing to curb the powers of Parliament, I think some way must be found to allow the CBC to operate free of political considerations, so long as it can operate with reasonable efficiency. Perhaps that's a tall order, but I don't think it's an impossible one.

The CBC has often been the victim of the government itself—and I don't mean just the Conservatives here, but the Liberals, too. One at least expects a Conservative government to be less committed to the idea of publicly financed broadcasting—the whole thing smacks of socialism, damn it all—but Liberal politicians have not been above sacrificing CBC health in the interest of more harmonious relations with recalcitrant backbenchers. The CBC is dependent on the government of the day both for its finances and the rules within which it operates. The government therefore has a responsibility to demonstrate its confidence in the *publicly* owned *national* broadcasting system by protecting it from political storms and regional greed.

As an example, take the matter of long-term financing. The second Fowler Report in 1967 recommended that the CBC be guaranteed its allowance of money for a longer period than one year at a time. This is something the CBC has been trying to get for years. But even when the advice came from a government-instigated Report, it went unheeded. It is impossible for the CBC to make any long-range plans when it must go to Parliament, hat in hand, each year to ask for money enough to keep operating. No broadcasting network in the United States could possibly operate this way. No big private company would be expected to operate this way. It just makes no sense at all.

When the government brought in its 1968 broadcasting legislation, it included a clause that would allow five-year financing. That is, the CBC would know that so many dollars would be available to it each year for the next five years.

This does not mean they would spend it like drunken sailors. It simply means they would know how far they could or could not go in long-range planning. The legislation bogged down in debate. Then, suddenly, the new broadcasting act was passed—but somehow the five-year financing clause had vanished.[1]

So once again the government—upon which the CBC depends—let the CBC down in order to placate the politicians who much prefer the firmer control they have by making the CBC come begging for money each year. That they are thereby hampering broadcasting does not seem to bother the politicians.

On another important matter, I find myself in disagreement with both the CBC and the Fowler Report. This is the question of originating more national broadcasting from the regions of Canada outside of the main production centres of Toronto and Montreal. I cannot fathom the Fowler Report's reasons for taking this stand, except that it sounds altruistic and non-partisan to want geographically representative CBC programming. The CBC's reasons for holding this view are easier to understand, but equally indefensible. CBC heads are constantly being pressured by their representatives in Winnipeg, Halifax, Vancouver and other centres to put more of their local or regional programs on the national network. There is no doubt that the politicians—both in and out of the House—have a hand in this.

In fairness—the pressure of these regional CBC representatives is quite natural. They feel pride in the work they do in their localities and would like all of Canada to be aware of it. And, of course, they in turn are pressured by local performers, writers, musicians and producers who want some national recognition. But I don't feel these reasons are good enough. It has been amply demonstrated in the United States and elsewhere that better television results from the concentration of production facilities in one or two main centres. I think the same can and should be done in Canada.

In the United States, the earlier years of television were marked by local developments in Chicago, Philadelphia,

---

[1]Some time later, I asked Judy LaMarsh about this. She told me the government had withdrawn this clause as the only way to insure passage of the legislation as a whole. "We had to withdraw it," she said, "or they'd still be stalling passage of the bill."

Detroit, St. Louis and other cities. But in time, this fizzled out (in so far as national network programming is concerned) and more and more production was moved to either New York or Hollywood. Today most of it originates in Hollywood, and New York remains the only other major network production centre.

This makes sense. New York has long been a theatrical centre, with a great pool of available talent, so much of the early TV programming originated there. Hollywood is the film capital, and as more and more TV shows shifted from live or video-tape to film, it was natural that production should centre on the west coast. All the cities in between now do virtually nothing but local or regional programming. Network production is done in Hollywood or New York—and the results are better.

I know that many people will oppose this view, especially when it is applied to Canada. What of the talented young singer in Regina? What happens to the bright director or designer in Vancouver, or the budding playwright in Moncton? Are they to be denied an opportunity simply because they are not living in Toronto or Montreal?

My answer to that is that Fred Astaire was not born on Broadway—he was born in Nebraska, and he went to New York. Bob Hope was not born in Hollywood; nor was Johnny Carson, nor Dean Martin, nor Harry Belafonte, nor the Smothers Brothers, nor Glen Campbell. Their talent and drive led them to seek out the places where they could have their opportunity and prove their worth.

The promising singer in Regina need not have an elaborate CBC station built in her neighborhood so that she can become a star without leaving home. If she cares enough, she will go where the action is. Naturally, if there is a local station in her city (public or private) she can gain some experience there. But she must eventually go to the place of greater opportunity if the career really matters to her. That

---

[1] Some years ago, George Burns, commenting on the decline of vaudeville and the young performer's problem of finding a few relatively obscure places to learn his trade, complained: "There's no longer any place to be lousy." But more recently, reminded of this comment, the veteran comedian reversed himself. "I've changed my mind about that," he said. "If there are places to be lousy, you'll stay lousy."

may be Toronto or Montreal or Hollywood or London. But they cannot come to her.[1]

I am not trying to discriminate against other Canadian cities, or to suggest that Toronto or Montreal are automatically *better*. But the fact remains that these are our biggest cities, the cities of cultural activity, of concentration of talent. They are the logical places for CBC network production centres, just as they are the logical places for more and better theatrical, musical and artistic achievement. I am not suggesting that existing CBC facilities in other cities should be closed down. Of course, they serve a purpose in providing local and regional programming, they employ local artists and craftsmen. Fine.

But if the CBC persists in this idea of originating more network programming from "the regions," inevitably this means expanding and improving the facilities in those cities (plus who knows how many more) at the expense of more urgently needed expansion and improvement in the two major production centres. The trouble is that the politicians—including the ones inside the CBC—view the CBC as a pie. Instead of thinking in terms of what is most likely to result in the best possible network programming, they each want a piece. They want handsome CBC structures in their cities, built by local contractors using local labor—all with funds from Ottawa. And they care not that by cutting up the pie they harm the cause of Canadian broadcasting.

The hapless CBC, like the victim of a blackmailer, must keep paying off—building better studios, expanding facilities, spending money in the most unlikely places in a desperate attempt to appease the politicians, in the forlorn hope that by so doing they will charm the politicians into allowing the CBC to go about its business otherwise unhampered. But who ever heard of charming a blackmailer?

As long as politicians are permitted to use the CBC as a football, as a source of revenue in the form of local installations, so long will the CBC be limiting its own potential by dissipating its resources rather than marshalling them. And the government is largely to blame for placing the CBC in such a vulnerable position. If the government and Parliament really cared about increasing the efficiency of the CBC, the long-talked-about CBC centre in Toronto would have been realized years ago. One has only to consider the money paid by the CBC for the various premises it rents to see how wasteful the present situation is.[1]

And, of course, with buildings scattered all over Toronto, there is the additional cost of transportation—a fleet of trucks and cars to transport people, cans of film, sets, costumes, props, papers, office supplies and whatnot from one part of the city to another. Since red tape breeds more red tape, the waste of money and effort become compounded—drivers for the cars, dispatchers, people to package the parcels that go from building to building, clerks to receive and record deliveries, office boys to distribute the parcels, receptionists to funnel them, and so on.

But, of course, the CBC can never seem to get the money all at once to build a proper centre in Toronto, in which all its various components could be consolidated. One of the chief reasons for this is the insistence that the CBC must spread the money around—placating a politician here and another one there by "improving" the facilities in dozens of areas across the country.

When the 1967 Fowler Report was published, much was made of one of its conclusions: "The only thing that really matters in broadcasting is program content—all the rest is housekeeping." The CBC promptly rejected this view, giving long-winded explanations of why all the "housekeeping" activities are essential to maintaining the CBC. One would have thought they should jump at this chance—handed them by the Fowler Report—to urge the granting of funds for consolidation of resources. But, no, the CBC has long since fallen into the trap of being on the defensive, compulsively rationalizing existing flaws.

I happen to agree here with Mr. Fowler. When an organization becomes as large and as spread out as the CBC, it is easier for departments within it to lose sight of what the whole Corporation is about. It resembles a harried bus driver who is running behind schedule; fearful of being criticized,

---

[1] Besides the studios and offices in the Jarvis-Mutual Street complex, there is Studio Four (the Pierce-Arrow Showroom) on Yonge Street. Then, there are offices in buildings on Gerrard Street, College Street, Maitland Street, Yonge Street, University Avenue, Church Street, a film department on Front Street, rehearsal halls and storage space on Sumach Street, plus probably a few more that I haven't yet discovered.

he races by people waving from street corners. In his zeal to get back on schedule, he ignores the fact that his primary function is to carry passengers. This pitfall is not one that is restricted to the CBC. It is a danger to any large organization. The trick is to recognize the fact that the pitfall exists and then to devise ways of avoiding it, rather than insisting publicly that there is no such trap.

The Fowler Report gives as an example (of too much stress on housekeeping) the fact that one can wander through the CBC's handsome headquarters building in Ottawa, passing through acres of desks, entering countless offices, all spotless and neat—and never even suspect what kind of business this headquarters runs. It is simply an office empire. This is equally true in Toronto and, I'm sure, in other cities where the CBC has installations. There are, by now, more receptionists, secretaries, typists, accountants, office boys, cleaning women, drivers, elevator operators, guards, clerks, executives and assistants in the CBC than there are people directly engaged in turning out radio and television programs.

Obviously, an organization so large must have many people in its employ. But the problem here is that sometimes the conditions, requirements, wishes, demands and activities of this army of supporting personnel tend to overpower that now smaller segment of the CBC still concerned with programming. And, I suppose, when you are the head of the whole organization, the demand of, say, a maintenance department head for forty new mops becomes as serious a problem as the demand for a new camera lens.

Labor relations might also be legitimately regarded as "housekeeping," and although I certainly don't suggest that the CBC has no need of such housekeeping activities, the danger remains of becoming so absorbed in these affairs as to lose sight of one's basic responsibility—in this case, as Mr. Fowler said, program content. This year, to cite a ludicrous instance, the Corporation felt compelled to print and circulate the details of a grievance meeting between its representatives (a committee of five) and those of the National Association of Broadcast Employees and Technicians (NABET).

First, the union's position was stated:

In the December issue of *Chatelaine,* CBC broadcaster Bruno Gerussi issued a threat to the safety of NABET Radio Technicians, in that he did threaten to "kick him in the clang." On searching the available literature on slang it was discovered that the word "clang" when used to describe human anatomical features is a colloquial illiteracy describing male genitalia. This threat, if carried to fruition would result in the ruination of the member's personal life and could even cause his death.

We thus demand that the Corporation live up to the meaning of Article 7.1.1. and eliminate working conditions which are a hazard to the health and safety of employees.

Then, the CBC's answer to this grievous complaint:
Management assures the union that it will make every effort to improve working conditions which are a hazard to the health of employees. Management recognizes the continuing concern of the union in promoting sound working relationships between technicians and performers. Management assures the union it will make every effort to promote such sound relationships for the mutual benefit of performers, technical staff and the Corporation.

This burning issue was settled peacefully, you'll be relieved to learn. The report of the grievance meeting didn't go into detail, but one can assume that Mr. Gerussi was duly warned to keep his non-NABET feet the hell away from the technician's clang, and thus the threat to the member's member never came to fruition.

Man, that's housekeeping.

I can give you a more serious and equally asinine example of the CBC's penchant for tidy housekeeping at the expense of more effective broadcasting.

In the CBC's radio building in Toronto, some of the microphones look (and sound) as if they were last used for the initial broadcast of The Happy Gang. I have been present on more than one occasion when grumbling producers and technicians bemoaned the fact that they are expected to get satisfactory results with such outdated equipment. But, of course, they have learned to live with the CBC's chronic poverty.

In the same building—a floor below the studios and near that singularly uninviting cafeteria that publicly-owned buildings seem to spawn—there is a men's lavatory in which the urinals are equipped with an electric-eye automatic flusher. No kidding—the moment you step back from the urinal it flushes, the mechanism being triggered by an electric-eye apparatus. I suppose the CBC figures its technicians are resourceful enough to make do with antique microphones, but they haven't got the sense to flush toilets manually. The unfortunate thing about this sort of thing is that it becomes increasingly difficult to persuade either the government or the public that the CBC should be given any more money when it has such a flair for mismanaging the amount it gets.

And I'm not just talking about a few microphones or an electric-eye flusher. There are other instances of CBC spending that are, to be charitable, questionable. I have in mind a certain panel show on which an orchestra of seven is employed to provide background and theme music which could easily be taken from the CBC's considerable library of recorded music. They are perfectly good musicians and I have nothing against them. But I know of no other panel show on television on this continent—except those game shows which deal specifically with identifying tunes and the like—on which live music is used.

This music accounts for about one thousand dollars of the program's weekly budget. Considering that the program is on the air for some forty weeks per year and that the series has been on the air for a dozen years, that's about $480,000 that has been spent on incidental (not to say irrelevant) music—largely because the CBC is reluctant to get into a dispute with the musicians' union.

The program started with live music, and the union takes the stand that as long as this particular program lasts, this condition may not be changed. I don't blame the union for protecting the interests of its members, but it shouldn't take an administrative genius to figure out that the CBC could by now have worked out a compromise with the union, whereby the band could be dropped from this particular program in exchange for which the Corporation could guarantee that an equal number of musicians (possibly even the same ones) would be used elsewhere in the CBC's programming.

Television budgets are always pretty tight in Canada, yet the CBC does sometimes move in a mysterious way its wonders to perform. I have in mind a particular program that is constantly strapped for money; and this ever-present budgetary limitation severely restricts the calibre of guests who may be approached to appear on the program. Yet, the producer of this same program takes several trips across Canada and into the United States each year, and every summer spends a few weeks in Europe—all at CBC expense on the flimsy excuse of "making contacts" for future programs in the series. He is not, in fact, unique. I know another producer who seems to travel extensively in the United States and Europe, presumably on CBC business. I have yet to see the fruits of his labor on my TV set.

But there are other, greater instances of the CBC's lopsided logic in divvying up the money it gets.

The CBC is not so much a big empire as a loose federation of little empires. These little empires vie with each other for favor—and money. There are times when interdepartmental in-fighting gets so petty that it is difficult to remember that they are all supposed to be parts of the same publicly-owned broadcasting corporation, pledged to serve the Canadian people.

Paradoxically, the light entertainment department, which has been instrumental in developing the few star names Canadian television can claim (Wayne and Shuster, Juliette, Tommy Hunter, Fred Davis, Bob Goulet) is perhaps the least powerful of the little empires.

For the past decade, it has become a kind of stepchild to the CBC. Except in local programming, the light entertainment department is expected to be revenue-producing and therefore is not free to put on programs it deems worthwhile unless they are sponsored.

Why the light entertainment department should be so regarded is something of a mystery, but I have my own theory as to the reason. The government feels reasonably secure about doling out money to a CBC which produces programs of news, public affairs, information or education, or programs that might be considered culturally or spiritually uplifting. But variety? Egad, that's show-biz and the opposition is always ready to ask what the hell the government is doing in show-biz. So, unless the variety department can justify its existence by bringing in revenue, its activities are curtailed. And it's always cheaper to buy Red Skelton or Hogan's Heroes.

Now, that may seem sensible and business-like to you, but not if you examine it in relation to expenditures in some other departments. Because the CBC is expected to do "cultural" programs, there have been instances where truly large sums of money have been spent on operas, ballets and classical dramas—which almost invariably go on the air unsponsored and are watched by a depressingly small segment of the public. I don't suggest there should be no such programming, of course, but considering that there are far more people who watch light entertainment than opera, a more realistic apportioning of departmental budgets might be taken into consideration.

The existing system results in some incredible inconsistencies. In 1968, a program called "Jazz Piano" was presented by the CBC. This was an uncommonly dull hour-"special" featuring four talented keyboard artists (Marian McPartland, Errol Garner, Bill Evans and a token Canadian, Brian Browne) reflecting different styles in piano jazz. It was produced by Special Programs or one of the other departments whose functions and boundaries are only vaguely defined. It would surely have been done better had it been produced by any one of half a dozen variety producers employed by the CBC. But it was not considered salable, and therefore the light entertainment could not do it. And so it was produced, rather ineptly and at a cost of something like twenty-five thousand dollars by a department that is not expected to bring in revenue. And so it went on the air—unsponsored, undistinguished, unnecessary.

Public Affairs is another department that gets preferential treatment (in comparison to light entertainment) by the CBC decision-makers. No one can quarrel with the importance of good and sufficient public affairs programming. But, again, CBC largesse to public affairs usually means tight money in other departments. And the freedom allowed public affairs—and I'm speaking here of freedom from want rather than freedom of speech—can sometimes encourage foolish spending.

Example: There was a Sunday afternoon series called "Today the World." I don't imagine it was too terribly expensive, considering that much of it consisted of films produced elsewhere and merely rented by the CBC. Still, I did think it odd when, last winter, a program in this series dealt with Lyndon Johnson's Washington. I'm not opposed to a program telling me all about Robert McNamara and Dean Rusk and the LBJ impact on Washington, but it did seem pointless to be watching such a program several weeks *after* the inauguration of Richard Nixon. The program had obviously been filmed and intended for showing months before, and whatever the CBC spent to get it was wasted money.

The CBC has long been interested in finding outside markets for some of its programs, and that makes sense because TV costs are so high that it's virtually impossible for programs to recover their costs in the limited Canadian market. Yet, the Corporation sometimes defeats its own purpose.

Example: A few years ago, the CBC entered into a cooperative venture with an outside producer (Maxene Samuels) to produce a series called "Seaway." A further financial contribution was made by British television interests, the idea being that the series would also be shown there. But, of course, the CBC was hoping for a sale to the United States, where the real money is. At one point, the CBC intended that the series should be done in color, but the British opposed this added cost, there then being little color TV in Britain. So the CBC gave in and produced the show in black and white. The series, despite some merit, failed to find any major market in the United States, specifically because it was not in color. At that time, color programs were in such great demand that almost any color program could have been sold. The same producer, again in association with the CBC, succeeded in selling a far less impressive series (Forest Rangers) in the United States largely because it was in color. So, in the case of Seaway, the CBC lost a substantial bundle of money by giving in to British pressure to keep the costs down by skipping the color—the same British who originated the term "penny wise and pound foolish."

Not all of my complaints about the CBC have to do with money, although money enters into many of them. Perhaps it has to do with size, perhaps with being an "institution," but I find the CBC tends to get into a rut and reject out of hand new ideas or new ways of meeting challenges. In practice, if not in politics, it is often rather conservative.

In the early days of television, the practice was established of promoting people from the ranks to positions of more authority and responsibility. There's nothing wrong with that concept, so long as it doesn't become too rigid a policy. In the CBC, a stagehand who proves his worth becomes a technician, then maybe a cameraman, then a studio director. Not every stagehand becomes a studio director, but most studio directors started as stagehands or technicians and worked their way up. The next step up for a studio director is usually producing. Again, not every studio director becomes a producer, but most producers were once studio directors. Of course, some such background and experience is helpful to a television producer. But it doesn't necessarily follow that this is the *only* acceptable background from which to draw producers. There are such things as creative ability, imagination, the talent for working with people—qualities not notably present in all studio directors.

I said much earlier in this book that the CBC tends to regard writers as a necessary evil. This may have seemed like a gross exaggeration, but I don't think it is. Anyway, it never seems to have occurred to the CBC that television writers might make good television producers. I find this rather remarkable in a medium of communication where writing is such a basic element, but in my twelve years or so of association with CBC light entertainment, I can think of only one or two instances of writers who were made producers. Can it really be that of all the writers who have worked for CBC variety in all that time, no more than that had the qualities to become valuable television producers? That hardly seems likely when you consider that the roster of former CBC variety or light entertainment writers includes people like Frank Peppiatt and John Aylesworth, Bernard Rothman, Saul Ilson, Allan Blye and Bernie Orenstein—all of whom moved on to Hollywood as television writers, and all of whom have since become television producers.

I don't claim that every television writer is a potential television producer. I don't claim that every producer who was once a writer is automatically better as a producer than one who never worked as a writer. But it is clear that the CBC does not consider writing background—television writing background—as valuable experience in choosing its producers. And I don't really think there's any conspiracy against writers. I think it's simply that the CBC has "always" looked to the studio crew for its potential producers rather than to writers, and the CBC doesn't seem to be aware that there are other directions in which to look. But it's also true, I'm afraid, that CBC officials tend to doubt their own judgment. And this seems to be most crucial when it comes to appraising the talents of creative people.

Since I have just mentioned Bernard Rothman, I will relate an incident concerning him. It illustrates all too clearly the lack of self-confidence in the CBC of which I speak. After gaining some theatrical experience in his native Montreal, Rothman moved to Toronto and became a studio director at CBC. He wanted to be a television producer but somehow there never seemed to be an opportunity for him. In time he gave up his staff job (CBC studio directors are on staff) and started writing on a free-lance basis for the CBC light entertainment department. After a couple of years of this, as the TV season was drawing to a close, he made inquiries as to what work there might be for him on summer shows. He was advised not to expect any summer assignment. Well, then, how about the fall? What prospects were there? Things didn't look too promising for the fall, either, he was told. The message got through to him: don't call us, we'll call you.

Rothman promptly wrote to a Canadian variety producer he knew who was then working in Australia, asking if there might be any work down there for the summer. A cable came back offering him a summer series at reasonably attractive money. Bernie, who was and is a friend of mine, mentioned to me that he was going to Australia to write for television there. At the time, I was still writing a show business column and I made mention of this bit of news in my column. The next day, Bernie was called by the CBC. The same man who had, a week or two earlier, given him a definite brush-off, now insisted that Bernie sign a contract for the fall—before leaving for Australia.

What did it mean? Simple: if someone in Australia wanted Rothman, Rothman must be good. Until someone else had made a judgment, the CBC wasn't really sure how good Rothman might be—even though his writing talents had already been employed by the CBC for a couple of years. As irrational as it sounds, it has happened too often at the CBC to be dismissed as an ironic little incident. But the CBC is not alone in this respect. Millions of Canadians are just as guilty.

Remember that long list of Canadian expatriates from theatre and television—John Vernon, Lorne Greene, Bob Goulet, William Shatner, Christopher Plummer, Gordon Pinsent, Lloyd Bochner, Larry Mann and so many others—all were taken for granted until they managed to gain the Hollyood or Broadway or London stamp of approval. That's when most Canadians suddenly showed some respect for them. And no matter how many times the point is made, nothing changes. Canadian sponsors and Canadian advertising agencies are no less guilty of the old Canadian inferiority complex. Ad agencies have for years spent much of their clients' money making commercials in the United States for showing in Canada—or else importing people from the States to film commercials here. (Some sponsors insist on this, but other times the agencies make the choice.)

One of the most maddening examples occurred early in 1969. Lorne Freed is a talented producer-director who spent several years at CFTO, working his way up to the key post of executive producer at the private Toronto station. At the end of 1968, he left the station to work as a free lance. Soon after, he was asked by an advertising agency to direct a commercial. It seems the agency had brought in a New York television director to do a series of commercials. He had botched the first one and was quickly dropped. Freed was asked to try one of the commercials. He did so well at it that the agency wanted to sign him to do all the remaining commercials in the series. Having worked for a small fee for the first commercial, Freed naturally now felt he was entitled to ask for substantially more for the rest of the series, having proven his worth. But when he named his figure, the agency people were aghast.

"That's crazy," they said. "Why, for that kind of money we could import a director from the States."

So, perhaps the CBC and the Canadian sponsors and the Canadian advertising agencies all reflect the Canadian viewpoint. Perhaps it is futile to find fault with the CBC, or with broadcasting practices or conditions in this country—without laying at least part of the blame on the Canadian public. If it's true that we get the kind of world we deserve—the kind of communities we deserve, the kind of business and labor, the kind of laws, the kind of government—then we also get the kind of television we deserve. And the only way we can expect it to improve is to decide that we *want* it improved.

But before we can make such a decision, maybe we have to know a little more about the basic reason it is the way it is. And that basic reason happens to be economics. So the time has come for a look at some of the pertinent economic facts of television.

The CBC or—What?

I guess that in the last chapter and some earlier ones I have been rather rough on the CBC. I have listed and detailed an assortment of complaints, a mixed bag of beefs. No doubt, if I had worked at CTV for a dozen years, or CBS or NBC or ABC or even BBC, I would have as many complaints— perhaps not all the same ones, but as many. However, I can write only from my own knowledge and experience and arrive at my own conclusions. Besides, it's not much help to wheeze a sigh of resignation and say, "Oh, well, these things are bound to happen in any big network—they're all the the same." I don't care about that. It's absolutely no consolation to me that CTV might be as bad or worse, or that ABC might be as tight-fisted or NBC as foolishly run. But I do care about the CBC—not only because I have seen it at close range, have worked with it, have worried over it—but mainly because I feel it plays a vital role in the life of Canada.

I don't think it's an overstatement to say that most Canadians are only dimly aware of how large a role the CBC has played in the life of this country. Historians generally credit the railroads with being in large measure responsible for both the development and the unification of Canada during this country's first half-century. The railways opened up new regions, pushed back our horizons. But they also linked together the existing communities, an achievement of at least equal importance. Broadcasting has performed a similar task during the second half of Canada's first century, as only broadcasting could do. In a country the size of Canada, the press could perform only a limited service in national terms. This is not meant to belittle the role of the press. It is simply not possible in so large a country to have a "national" newspaper, the claims of Toronto's morning newspaper to the contrary notwithstanding.

Only broadcasting could truly link the people of the east coast with those of the west—and all of the people in between. Only broadcasting could tell people in one part of the country what is happening *now* in another part. And to the extent that broadcasting was national, this meant the CBC. I know about the many privately owned stations that have, and they still do exist; but for the most part they serve their own communities or, at best, their regions. However noble their intentions or ingenious their methods, whatever their claims, private radio stations could not have afforded to provide a national radio broadcasting service in Canada in the same sense that the CBC did. The same, naturally, is true of television—only more so. Television is a terribly expensive business and it takes a substantially larger population to support it, in the fashion that private enterprise is accustomed to, than Canada can yet offer.

I know that for years private broadcasters have been telling us—often through the newspapers which some of them also happen to own—that if they were allowed to, they could do what the CBC does and do it better and also show a profit. And private businessmen, who resent paying taxes to support a CBC, have joined in the chorus, encouraging the private broadcasters in this stand.

But it just isn't so. The same businessmen (sponsors) who spent a decade moaning about the damn CBC have not shown themselves to be overly generous or co-operative in their dealings with private broadcasters. Far from it. The reasons are economic. The fact is that very few sponsors have ever paid the CBC the full cost of any program they have "sponsored." In order to lure sponsors the CBC has had to devise strange ways of arriving at attractive price tags for programs it offers to sponsors.[1] That price tag doesn't necessarily include such items as the salary of the producer, who is under contract to the CBC, or the studio director or

---

[1] Even more devious methods are employed. If a Canadian advertiser wants to sponsor an American program on the CBC, the Corporation will try to horse-trade with him—agreeing to import the program only if the sponsor will also pay for a Canadian program. Deflating though it may be to the Canadian artist's ego, that's the only basis on which some Canadian programs get any sponsorship at all.

production assistants, or the true cost of many other elements that go into a television production.

The price to the sponsor does not really take into account the CBC's overhead costs. It is arrived at largely on the basis of what is called "direct money"—that is, money actually paid out to non-staff people hired specifically for the program, such as singers, musicians, actors, writers—plus an estimate of the "indirect" costs—money paid in salaries by the CBC for stagehands, carpenters, electricians, secretaries, et cetera. This latter item presumably covers overhead, but it does not in fact reflect the true overhead costs of running the CBC. If it did, no sponsor would be caught dead within a mile of a CBC show. What this means is that if a sponsor of a CBC show pays ten thousand dollars a week for a program, that program is actually costing the CBC half again as much, in some cases twice as much, perhaps even more. The CBC does not do this out of generosity or naivety. The motivation is a realistic appreciation of the factors involved. The CBC knows how much a sponsor can be persuaded to spend; and the sponsor himself knows how much he should spend in relation to what he gets out of it.

But, inevitably, the Canadian sponsor has been spoiled. When a private network or an independent producer approaches a Canadian sponsor with a program, he is forced to compete with those unreal CBC rates. The private broadcaster or independent producer cannot "hide" or juggle his costs. He gets no handout from Parliament to enable him to produce programs or equip stations. He must put a true price tag on his program, and unless he cuts a lot of corners he cannot possibly put on a program for the same price that the CBC charges the sponsor. He can come up with "a program," but the economic limitations imposed on it usually prevent it from being on a par with what the CBC is capable of doing. I'm not being biased in favor of the CBC in this; the same problem usually prevents the CBC's programs from being as impressive or ambitious as those done in the United States, where the economic factors are far less restrictive.

The key fact about television production is cost. There is no getting away from this, whether you are talking about CBC or CTV or any other network. Television production means not only good ideas and good planning; it usually means attrative production values—sets, costumes, music, et cetera—and these cost money. And most of all, perhaps, it means adequate rehearsal—and that costs money. The more you try to cut corners, the more you risk destroying the very values that make the program attractive to public and sponsor.

When a private broadcaster approaches a sponsor with a program idea, he brings it in at the lowest possible price he can sensibly offer. Let us say it is a simple game or panel show, to cost six or seven thousand dollars a week. The sponsor—the same one who has been cursing the CBC for years—shakes his head: "Why should I pay you so much, when I can get the same show from the CBC for four thousand dollars?" However betrayed the private broadcaster may feel, there isn't much he can do about it. Except cut more corners.

It is ironic that the same factor—cost—which makes the sponsors shy away from the CBC, thus keeping it in the red, often forces private television producers to turn out inferior programs and thus make sponsors shy away from them, too. But the factor is a real one and cannot be made to go away just because we don't like it. To appreciate this, it might be helpful to examine briefly the basis on which sponsors decide what they can or cannot spend on television advertising.

The yardstick is the "cost per thousand" system—that is, the sponsor (or his chosen advertising agency) can easily figure out how much he can sensibly afford to pay out to lure each one thousand viewers. This guides him in deciding whether or not a particular program should get his financial support. In the United States, where television costs are somewhat higher than they are in Canada, the sponsor can still afford to pay for far more expensive shows. If the network producing or distributing Bonanza or the Dean Martin Show goes to a sponsor and offers such a program for one hundred and fifty thousand dollars a week (and in today's TV world that's not an extravagant estimate) the sponsor will likely buy it.

Let's say the sponsor is General Motors or Lever Brothers, to name two likely candidates. (These days, more and more programs have several sponsors rather than one, but that doesn't change things—it's merely a matter of splitting the costs.) The sponsor (or sponsors) will buy the program because he knows that through such a program he can reach probably twenty million viewers each week—at a cost of seven dollars and fifty cents per thousand viewers. Think about that: it would cost the sponsor seven-tenths of a penny to persuade each viewer to buy a bar of soap. Not a bad bargain for an advertiser.

Now let's move back to Canada. Let's say that because our television costs are lower here (no big star salaries to pay, for example) the CBC or CTV could produce an equivalent program at half the cost—seventy-five thousand dollars a week instead of one hundred and fifty thousand dollars. Frankly, I doubt if it could be done at so low a cost, but just for the sake of argument let's say it's possible. The network goes to General Motors of Canada or Lever Brothers Limited with such a proposition. Either sponsor—or any other one, for that matter—would surely turn it down. And he would be right.

The reason is obvious. With Canada having only ten per cent of the population that the United States has, what the sponsor can expect of his program is to reach about two million viewers. The "cost per thousand" is much higher if you spend seventy-five thousand dollars a week to reach two million people than if you spend one hundred and fifty thousand dollars to reach twenty-million—five times as high, to be precise. The soap maker would now be spending three and three-quarters cents to persuade each viewer to buy a bar of soap. And that is not very good business thinking. So despite the belief that television costs are lower in Canada, they are actually lower in the United States, in relation to a sponsor's ability to pay those costs based on the size of the TV audience he can influence.

Population is the key to the whole problem. Because of the huge population (translation: market) in the United States, television sponsors can afford to spend far more money to buy programs, and television producers and networks can therefore spend a lot more on their programs. Television is an expensive business and a country as sparsely populated as ours simply cannot afford to spend the kind of money on TV that the United States can—the CBC can't afford it, and CTV is even farther from being able to afford it.

So, what's the answer? I guess it's a matter of choice. The people of Canada have to make up their minds—if they can be prodded into thinking about it at all—about what matters to them. One choice, and probably the easiest, is simply to forget about Canadian television. Pack up the CBC, sell its studios and cameras to private stations and networks, and let the government get the hell out of broadcasting once and for all.

Let's suppose we did this. Starting tomorrow, the CBC is no more. CTV, or CTV and a second private network, now own or operate all the television stations across Canada. Apart from a possible reduction in taxes (Hooray!) what will we have accomplished? What will the private networks do once the CBC is out of their way? What would they be able to do that they cannot do now? Has the market increased? Are there any more Canadians available to watch television and buy soap? Will the cost of a program be any less to the sponsor, and thus enable him to spend more to get better programs? Of course not. Nothing has changed significantly. Perhaps CTV will draw four million viewers for a program instead of two million, because their competition will have been eliminated. But that's only true until a second private network moves in and again splits the market.

So the economic limitations would remain. The private stations and networks—no subsidy from the taxpayers now, remember—will still have to cope with the problem of competing with American programs and, at the border points where millions of Canadians live, even with American stations. So the logical next step for them is to bring pressure to bear on the Canadian Radio and Television Commission, or whatever body might some day suceeed it, to lower or even drop altogether the requirement that Canadian television stations must carry a certain minimum of Canadian programming. They will demonstrate convincingly before the Commission that they cannot afford to produce Canadian programs that are sponsorable and still be able to show a profit—or, at least, break even. They will insist that their only hope of survival as businesses is to cut drastically the amount of Canadian programming they are required to put on the air.

In all likelihood, in time the broadcasting regulatory body will give in to such arguments. They will cut down the fifty-five per cent Canadian content requirement—or maybe juggle it around in such a way that it is meaningless. And we'll all get a happy diet of imported programs—not only Ed Sullivan and Dean Martin, but also The Flying Nun and Gilligan's Island and Felony Squad and It Takes A Thief and Gomer Pyle and Doris Day and Bewitched and Jackie Gleason and Carol Burnett and Mission Impossible and reruns of Lucy and Danny Thomas and Dick Van Dyke and I Spy and The Man From Uncle and just about any other program from the States you can think of, good or bad, old or new.

All of them are available; many of them are now seen in Canada, on one or another of the networks. All I'm saying is that we're going to get a hell of a lot more of them. We get them now and we'll get more of them because with very few exceptions it is far less expensive for a Canadian network or station to import a U.S. show than to produce a Canadian one. And as the number of imported programs rises, the number of Canadian shows will decrease. In time, there will be no Tommy Hunter or Telescope, no Don Messer or Front Page Challenge, no River Inn or It's Happening, no Man At The Centre or Wojeck, no Newsmagazine or Pierre Berton, no Vanda King or Juliette, no Under Attack, maybe even no Canadian football.

Well, okay. Would that be the end of the world? No. It wouldn't be the end of the world if there were no Canadian television programs at all. It wouldn't be the end of the world if there were no Canadian Opera Company. It wouldn't be the end of the world if there were no Stratford Festival. It wouldn't be the end of the world if there were no Charlottetown Festival. It wouldn't be the end of the world if there were no National Ballet of Canada, or Royal Winnipeg Ballet. It wouldn't have been the end of the world if there had been no Expo 67. It wouldn't be the end of the world if there were no Manitoba Theatre Centre. It wouldn't be the end of the world if there were no Toronto or Montreal or Edmonton or Halifax or Vancouver symphony orchestras, or no National Youth Orchestra. It wouldn't be the end of the world if there were no Dominion Drama Festival or Canadian Repertory Theatre. It woudn't be the end of the world if there were no Place des Arts in Montreal or National Arts Centre in Ottawa. It wouldn't be the end of the world if there were no National Gallery of Canada. But it sure as hell would be the beginning of the end of Canada.

In this country, perhaps even more so than in some others because of our sparse population, the arts cannot exist without financial support from the public. This is recognized in the existence of the Canada Council, the Ontario Arts Council and similar bodies. It is recognized in every city that holds a bazaar or a drive for funds to keep its symphony orchestra or its theatre alive. It is recognized in the campaigns that go on annually to raise money for art galleries, music schools, drama festivals.

But no area of Canadian artistic or cultural activity is as vulnerable as television. Simply because the costs are so high and the market too small to be profitable—and because the public and the government do not grant it the same status as theatre, music, ballet, et cetera—the temptation to turn over our air waves completely to the easily and inexpensively procurable imported shows is great. Only the continued existence of a government-backed body which regulates the amount of permissible imported programming can keep broadcasters from making their stations merely extensions of American networks or distributors.[1]

However, I said this was a matter of choice. I think the people of Canada must decide what is important to them. Those of us who are or have been actively involved in television tend to lose sight of the fact that while to us it is a way of life, to the public it's a matter of far less concern. To most people, television is merely a diversion, a harmless form of relaxation. It's there. You flick on the switch and gaze absently at whatever is on. If you like it, fine. If not, you simply switch to another channel—or turn the set off.

---

[1] Even the CBC is not above bending the rules in order to maintain its Canadian content level up to the required minimum. A program such as Cinema Six, which shows imported feature films, would normally be classed as non-Canadian. But the CBC uses the device of a "host" who introduces the film and talks about it for some five minutes before it starts. Miraculously, the full two hours or so of the film's running time is now classified as "Canadian content." That's how lenient broadcasting regulations are already.

Most people watch programs they like (or are used to) with no thought as to whether they are Canadian or imported. That is their right, of course, and it's also what we call human nature. But it is this very lack of interest that poses a problem as to the future of Canadian television. It may very well be that most people don't really give a damn whether there's a CBC or a CTV or whether forty or fifty-five per cent or ninety-five per cent of our programs are piped in from the States or anywhere else. I suppose, to follow the argument through, it may be that many people don't give a damn whether this country is to survive as an entity for another century or be gradually absorbed into the social, economic, cultural and political life of the United States. It's a chilling thought to some, of course, but the possibility is there. But if there are Canadians who do care, who do feel that the future identity of this country is important, and that identifiably Canadian programming *is* a vital factor in the preservation of that identity, then those people have an obligation to do something about it.

Why should they bother? Simply because a passive attitude in this instance has the effect of supporting the opposite view—the view that television in this country doesn't matter, even perhaps that the future existence of Canada does not matter. To sit back idly is not merely to remain neutral, but to support the opposite side. And just what is it that I would have Canadians do to prove their concern? What action do I recommend that will "save" the Pierce-Arrow Showroom?

First of all, it's a question of attitude. We must try to get over this habit of sniping at the CBC, harassing it, resenting it, shackling it, cursing it at the same time that we accept its offerings. After all, the politicians who thrive on needling the CBC do it not only because they know this is a way of attracting attention—especially in a decidedly anti-CBC oriented press—but also because they know it's a way of pleasing their more gullible constituents. Hardly a month goes by any more when there isn't some orator on his feet in the House of Commons complaining about too much violence on television, or too much ballet, or too much money being spent, or too many Separatists being allowed on the air, or too many hippies, or too many radicals, or too much sex, or too much something.

Such politicians are sustained and encouraged by those people who feel compelled to write angry letters denouncing the CBC for something they saw, or didn't see. I find it rather sad that in a world with problems like Vietnam, Biafra, racial injustice, poverty and crime, so many Canadians can get so worked up over Gordon Sinclair's question to a young swimmer about menstruation. And I find it unutterably provincial that the president of the CBC should be obliged to go before the House of Commons to defend the Corporation over such trivia. I think it is ridiculous that the CBC, virtually alone among public services, should be subjected to the kind of picayune, hair-splitting, obstructionist tactics that pass for unbiased reportage of its activities in our press, which so often has more than a passing vested interest in broadcasting. We spend countless millions on a multitude of government services, most of which we neither understand nor question. But we balk at paying for a national broadcasting service—partly because we have been tricked into believing that if the government weren't involved such a service would be "free."

Our papers gleefully play up the alarming statements by politicians about the seemingly astronomical figures spent on or by the CBC. And when the CBC or the government point out that what the service is costing us amounts to eight dollars a year per person, we dismiss that as being irrelevant. We ignore the fact that whether we do it through taxes for the CBC or the price of products advertised on television we are still paying for our television, as are the viewers of any other country. We prefer to think they (in the United States, for example) are getting their television for nothing. And we still harbor the vague notion that if we could only get rid of all those bureaucrats and the weirdo CBC types with beards and sandals and put broadcasting into the hands of hard-nosed businessmen, everything would work out dandy.

Let us get it straight once and for all: private enterprise in Canada cannot afford to give us worthwhile Canadian television and also show a profit. And, believe me, the latter goal is more important to them than the former. I am not attacking or decrying the profit motive. I am simply stating what is so: television cannot be profit-making in this country if it is to concern itself with maintaining any respectable level of worthwhile Canadian programming. The population —the "market"—is just too small to pay for it.

So, then, here are the choices I see: If you feel it does not matter whether or not there is to be any significant Canadian television in the future, then vote for politicians who would abolish the CBC, save yourself eight dollars a year in taxes, do away with "Canadian content" requirements and let our television consist primarily of imported programs. But if you feel the future of distinctively Canadian television does matter to this country, then accept the inevitability of the CBC—however improved or reformed—and allow it the freedom from economic and political pressure it needs to survive. In short, stop whining and pay the taxes.

I can think of only one other alternative, and that is that every able-bodied man and woman in Canada should go to bed tonight and try to make a baby. If this procedure is repeated and continued for a couple of years, in a generation we may have a population large enough to be able to support the television habit without either paying taxes to finance a CBC or relying on imported programs. If this last suggestion strikes you as facetious or impractical, then you can dismiss it and go back to a choice between the other two. I just thought a third choice might be interesting to explore. But I think we must recognize that we can't have it both ways. We can't have our Canadian content and show a profit, too. Time is growing short. Even the CBC, fed up with the dilemma of trying to keep peace with everyone—including the penny-pinching public and the carping press—is showing more and more signs of selling what's left of its tattered soul.

Take, for instance, the matter of Laugh-In. This highly successful program was carried by the CTV network for two seasons. The private Canadian network was paying NBC (who distribute the show) about eight thousand dollars a week during the 1968/69 season, an increase of about one thousand dollars a week from the previous season. In the spring of 1969, when deals are made for the following season, CBC outbid CTV for Laugh-In and bought the American show for Canada for the 1969/70 season. Estimated price: fifteen thousand dollars a week. Obviously, CTV had gone as high as it felt it could. Just as obviously, CBC was in a position to bid substantially higher. So now a popular American program that was already being seen on the private Canadian network is now being seen on the publicly-financed Canadian network.

I'm sure audiences in Canada don't really care which station Laugh-In is on, so long as they can see it. But does it make sense that the CBC should be paying so much to import an American program which was already available to many Canadians—and to do so at a time when the CBC itself is cutting back on Canadian light entertainment programs, largely because of lack of funds to produce them? There are not many Canadian light entertainment shows that cost fifteen thousand dollars a week—on either Canadian network.

It seems to me there is a kind of admission of defeat in the CBC's action. At the very least, it shows a deplorable lack of initiative and imagination. It suggests that the CBC is giving up the fight, saying: "Oh, the hell with it. Why should we bother to put together programs that are tough to sell when we can buy this? Why should we try to originate variety shows only to have the press shoot them down?" But what is more important is that the CBC is ignoring one of its basic responsibilities—to the public; and to hell with the press. That responsibility is to provide Canadian programming of all kinds, to suit all tastes at different times.

There are not many areas of programming left in which Canadian artists can find a television outlet. If the CBC is allowed—or forced—to dissolve yet another one, the future of television in this country looks gloomy indeed. Nobody, not the CBC nor the Canadian Radio and Television Commission nor the timid government which gives lip service to the principle of a CBC, will do anything to change this course unless they are given some indication that a substantial segment of the Canadian public wants something done.

What the CBC desperately needs now is a transfusion—a transfusion of confidence from the Canadian people and the Canadian government. Then, perhaps, that confidence will grow stronger inside the CBC and enable it to begin again acting like a professional broadcasting network instead of a panic-stricken rabbit. I don't think, therefore, that I'm just being an alarmist when I say as I did at the outset that the

Pierce-Arrow Showroom is leaking and no one is on duty. Canadian television is leaking and unless someone decides to report for duty soon to plug the leaks, it's only a matter of time before the whole question will become academic.

It may seem relatively unimportant that Laugh-In should replace Show of the Week. It may be of no concern to you that Festival dies and gives way to another ninety-minute filmed Hollywood drama. Perhaps you even think it insignificant that in hockey, a Canadian game in which almost one hundred per cent of the players are Canadian, the game and its TV coverage are moving towards domination by American ownership and American broadcasting "requirements." Will it matter to you, I wonder, when you turn on your set one night and instead of Stanley Burke or Harvey Kirck you see—live, in color, from New York—Walter Cronkite or Huntley and Brinkley?

But I've gone too far. I'm exaggerating, surely. That could never happen.

Or could it?